YOUR

ACCOUNTANT

The Good, the Bad
and the Greedy

Chris Rowland Thomas BA FCA

YOUR ACCOUNTANT

The Good, the Bad

and the Greedy

Published by

YOUR BOOKS PUBLISHING LTD

Merton Abbey Mills, London SW19 2RD

First published 2016

Copyright © 2016 – Chris Rowland Thomas

chrisrowlandthomas@gmail.com

ISBN 978-0-9955256-0-3

ABOUT THE AUTHOR

Chris Rowland Thomas BA(Hons) FCA has been an accountant in public practice for over thirty years. He founded his own firm the day after he qualified and is now the senior partner of Thomas Harris Chartered Accountants. Based in South London, the firm numbers amongst its clients many celebrities, musicians and actors as well as ordinary businesses and self-employed individuals. In 2016 the firm was voted 'Best Celebrity Tax Advisors' in the AI Tax Awards.

CONTENTS

Introduction

1 The good accountant

2 The Wild West

3 Chartered

4 Choosing

5 Judgement

6 Tied-up

7 Fees

8 Overcharging

9 Advice

10 Service

11 Self-employed

12 Directors

13 Investigations

14 Favouritism

15 Keeping down costs

16 Being proactive

17 Chaos theory

18 Bad guys

19 Troubleshooting

20 Good or bad?

INTRODUCTION

Over seven million people in the UK use the services of a practising accountant. Government statistics show that five million of these are business owners, with 99% being small businesses. The rest are made up of individuals or personal clients. You'd think this would mean a competitive fair market for accountancy services. The truth is different.

You should be able to shop around for services and fees, compare firms and, above all else, have a choice. In today's world the internet offers you guidance, price comparisons, reviews and in theory a basis for choice. But for these millions of users it is not a free market and there is no meaningful guidance on the internet or elsewhere.

Accountants know how to exploit the way in which their particular discipline operates in the UK's financial environment. The system is regulated by a mixture of statutes and the self-regulated rules of the various governing bodies. Accountants know the complex rules, clients don't. But the clients are forced to play, to gamble if you like – to pick up the dice and roll.

'I was recommended to my accountant' you might say. But what does that amount to? When you analyse it, not a lot. In fact, it can work against you.

Much is written about the 'Big Four' giant accountancy firms, carving out vast fees from audit and tax avoidance, but not so much about others who exploit the smaller clients trapped in a system where they have to use the services of the accountants they cannot properly judge or select on an informed basis. I am going to explain what you can do within this system to evaluate your accountant, move towards the best service, good advice, tax saving and reasonable fees, and to weed out the bad and find the good.

CONFUSION

The word 'accountant' in the UK embraces a number of disciplines, which accounts for its substantial membership of over 300,000, dwarfing family doctors at a mere 50,000 and solicitors at 118,000. It covers management accountants, tax advisors, auditors, liquidators, commerce and public practice. This all-embracing nature of the profession creates public confusion. Other countries define the profession more narrowly: for example, in the US you are either a CPA (Certified Public Accountant) or nothing. In Germany it is split into four or five different tiers. In the UK we just have 'accountants', with masses of available professional acronyms and seven regulating bodies with different titles.

The UK system, which once led the world, has now become impossible for the public to understand. The law actually allows the unregulated guy with no accountancy training to set up in the high street and compete with the professionally qualified and regulated firms – and the client is none the wiser. Gulp. This makes a mockery of the regulating bodies. The qualified are required to have insurance, ongoing training, regular monitoring and file inspection, to make sure they are doing the basics. Whereas anybody else with none of these costs, or any training whatsoever, can register as an advisor with HM Revenue and Customs, ask clients for their money laundering IDs and look respectable. So we have ended up with a messy game of chance where so-called accountants have the rule book and the public have to play blind.

FEES

As for the thorny question of accountants' fees, practising accountants have a system that operates outside a fair market. Fees can vary from one accountant to another by an amazing 500% for the same work. Even more astounding is that the service and advice you may get from the most expensive can be inferior to the service from the cheapest. What kind of regime is this that allows this to happen? It is going against the very essence of free market capitalism. Why are fees so unfairly dished out? Well, forget about the 'why' for now – let's be practical and get on the path to fairer fees.

One extreme comment on an internet forum about accountants' fees, said this:

> As an experienced accountant, I can say without hesitation that the majority of the accountants are obliging idiots and 100% of the auditors are greedy and dishonest buggers, and would (do) anything to cook up clients' accounts to get fat.

But accountants are far from idiots. Some have first-class degrees and most who are properly qualified have passed really tough exams. Accountancy is about making money, it is not social work and the purveyors can excel at it. The best, with a winning smile and a smart suit, turn money-making into their vocation. Practising accountants develop great PR skills and become adept at managing client expectations to create fees. Clients come and go, with the accountant maximising his fees at every opportunity. You are caught up in a financial lottery rigged against you. You meekly buy your ticket in the vain hope your number will come up. Unfortunately it won't, but you cling on to that hope, that dream. The dream that you have picked a winning accountant and his advice is sacrosanct. He seems such a nice guy and was recommended. Many have learnt the hard way.

ADVICE

All clients want the best in advice on their affairs. But how do you know if it's good advice or not? In 90% of cases you don't. So you will need to know how to look at other signs, not the taste of the coffee and biscuits (in fact that can be a bad sign) but the solid things that do matter. Your approach can make the difference between your accountant being proactive or not; between getting the 'bog standard' treatment or getting him to go that extra mile for you.

It's a murky world where one accountant's advice can save you thousands while another's can cost you dearly. So, what can you do?

YOUR GUIDE

This book will guide you and give you inside knowledge to put you more ahead of the game. You will be able to take more control and by your actions and people-skills mould your accountant into that good one you want. So get ready to turn the tables and receive the best in advice, service and tax saving coupled with fair charging. You can dip in or dip out of the chapters that are right for you. The first part of the book sets the scene and then the chapters develop into your practical guide to getting that good guy, and not the bad and the greedy.

<u>Note</u>

For simplicity's sake, I have used the masculine throughout when referring to the hypothetical accountant, i.e.'him', 'his', 'he', 'guy' etc., but this should in all cases be taken to include a reference to the female/LGBT equivalent.

1

THE GOOD ACCOUNTANT

Welcome to this book which takes you on a journey into the inner world of chartered accountants in public practice, immortalised in a classic *Monty Python* sketch, where *John Cleese* describes the accountant as:

> [an] appallingly dull fellow, unimaginative, timid, spineless, easily dominated, with no sense of humour, tedious company and irrepressibly drab and awful.

It gets worse. All these characteristics are, he continues, a boon to being an accountant. This is the accepted stereotype and we have swallowed it. TV has a lot to answer for in this. The result is that when you come across an apparently normal, charming and knowledgeable accountant in professional practice, you are amazed that he exists, you think you have bagged a good one. When his PR skills convince you he knows his stuff and that he is going to apply this expertise for you – you are sold. Or as some might say 'stitched up'.

Everyone wants that personable and effective accountant and (as we will see) these boring nonentities can metamorphose from the stereotype into a God-like being who can solve your problems. They have quite a few cards stacked in their favour:

- The client is often undergoing a new and unique experience.
- Professionals are assumed to be in possession of mysterious 'secrets' that it takes years to understand and these superior beings seem to know all the answers.
- They have the backing of a respected and long-standing institution.
- They know you need an accountant, and can be pretty confident you will buy the product.
- They are more often than not quite clever and shrewd.
- They know you can be convinced you have a good accountant before they do any work.

THE CREATIVE JUICES

However, even though the *Monty Python* image paints them as a rather dull and an uncreative bunch you would be astonished to find just how creative accountants can get when it comes to their own affairs and indeed some 'favoured' others.

When I first started in this game, there was a way that you could reduce your personal business tax by an incredible 50% with advance planning. Yes, your tax bill, whatever it was, could be virtually halved. Accountancy firms did it for their own benefit initially. It involved a five-year plan where the profits of two years out of five simply vanished from the taxation equation. So you made sure you manipulated the major profits into those years. All totally legal. Those firms would then extend this planning to family and friends. I did it for my girlfriend when I was a trainee.

It took the Revenue years to close this loophole down by which time accountants had saved millions for themselves and their 'favoured' clients. Normal clients had no knowledge of this simple, totally legal and effective scheme. This is just one example, but the creative treatment does not need to be this complex or spread over five years.

My business partner and I get together two or three times a year to talk about the future and in particular what our tax liabilities will be. Tax is a big expense and you plan to minimise it. (Let's leave the morality issue aside for now.) Our creative juices are flowing. We look at everything we do within the law to maximise our take-home pay. And it makes a substantial difference. All accountants will do this for themselves, their relatives... and who else?

Simple acts of creativity directed in your direction can save you thousands. So are you getting the timid spineless treatment or have you got that **good accountant** clients dream about?

WHAT IS 'GOOD'?

Every accountant will claim to be a 'good' accountant. Their websites will tell you how 'good' they are, how they can do all the standard things like accounts, tax returns and company formations. It's a bit like a school brochure saying 'We teach reading and arithmetic'. Some will go a stage further and say they do 'tax planning' – a wonderful phrase for the accountant, great fun. **Tax planning** – isn't that what everybody wants? Some clients will think this accountant is one up on the rest when the reality is he is one up on their PR. The phrase 'tax planning' covers anything from telling you how much you have to pay in two months' time, which all accountants should do anyway, to moving all your business interests into trusts and tax havens. This is vast territory, so wide open as to be meaningless.

Then there are the huge accountancy fees that can be generated by convincing clients to go into dodgy tax schemes. Accountants poured their top clients into them, clients told their friends what great and good accountants they had (recommendations) and their friends came in. An hour spent convincing an esteemed musician, accidently born being able to sing in tune, could generate an extra £200,000 in fees. *George Michael*, the singer, is reported to have paid £443,000 in fees to shelter some £6 million in such a scheme. I would hazard a guess, but that could equate to fees of some £10,000 per hour for the accountants/advisors. The unscrupulous would sell their mother for that.

I am pleased to say that I never asked one of my clients to go into these, despite the opportunities. In fact I positively discouraged them. These schemes on the whole were in fact only tax deferral schemes, that means a saving now but you will have to pay it later, but this was never really explained to the clients. Members of such schemes are feeling the HMRC backlash now with serious effects on their finances.

There will be other claims like 'We are proactive accountants'. Really? And what exactly is that? Do you call every month when we don't need it and charge us for that? Or do you sell us other irrelevant services, covert us to limited companies when we would be better off without, or put Rottweiler-type financial advisors on to us? (I go into more detail of what a proactive accountant should really do for you in Chapter 16.)

Then there are testimonials, the scourge of the internet. Surely if others like them, then as a potential client you can't go wrong. Whereas on *Trip Advisor* you get good and bad, the accountants' disgruntled clients generally keep shtum, having quietly moved on to pastures new, keeping the bad choice they made to themselves. So these random positive testimonials lack the independence accountants (auditors) are famed for, and are ultimately meaningless.

Some accountants even reel out their A-Z list celebrities in order to hook aspiring wannabes who think that by using the same accountant as other successful people, some of that fame is going to rub off on them.

The press will often make reference to a 'good' accountant. Usually they just mean 'big'. In their eyes, *PwC* (*Price Waterhouse Coopers*, one of the Big Four) is the proverbial big/good accountant, but actually it's a massive money-making machine where its highly intelligent partners have worked their heads off for years to get into the position where they can exploit the brand and make megabucks for themselves.

ADVICE

So why do we want good advice from a good accountant? Because it will generally lead to:

(a) paying less in tax
(b) higher business profits
(c) more money in your pocket
(d) save you from financial disaster

In extreme cases, bad advice, on the other hand, will act negatively on all these issues.

If you ask people how to get that right advice, most will say, 'Get yourself a good accountant.' By 'good', people generally mean a high-quality or excellent accountant. But does good mean costly, and vice versa? When you are talking about accountancy services, you assume you are going to have to pay serious money to get top quality and excellence. People infer good advice cannot be got on the cheap, and that if you cut corners on price you will end up with bad advice.

I once went to see an accountant in London who was retiring. He was in fact a Board of Trade Auditor – a regulated auditor who had never done any accountancy exams. Basically, it means he had been doing the job for years and was authorised because of that. He met me at the door and asked me into the front room of his terraced house. He had slippers on and stood in front of an electric bar fire. His prices were so cheap I could not believe it, and because he was such an inoffensive 'nice' guy clients warmed to him. It quickly became clear, however, that he had no up-to-date knowledge, no back-up, no library, no computer and probably did not even use a calculator. So what exactly was the quality work he was doing for his clients? And how many clients got his advice cheaply but paid more tax than they should have? Of course, nobody knows.

It may well be that if you go 'on the cheap' then you will get bad advice. 'You get what you pay for,' people always say. But is this true for accountancy services?

Unfortunately it is not just a case of paying through the nose to get the best. You may get trapped in a situation where overpayment is the norm and you are getting mediocre advice – textbook stuff. If you are getting that service and it combines with other factors that may irritate your accountant (see later chapters for these) you might be in for an even rougher ride. And that can cost you quite a lot of money in certain circumstances.

QUALITY

Look, if you want a high-quality, excellent car you might choose a new *Mercedes*. Not many would dispute that you have a good car. In accountancy services, though, you just don't know what you are getting for your money. You may buy into a brand – *PwC*, for example, or the more generic *Chartered Accountants* – but what continuity are you getting from the actual firm, and where is the accountability? More of that later.

When you get that new *Mercedes* you assume, with a pretty high degree of certainty, that the car will meet high standards. You will expect that every aspect of how that car interfaces with you, the customer, has been meticulously planned. You know it is expertly designed, properly manufactured, quality controlled and customer checked. You are aware that the dealership has reports and feedbacks from you about the car and service. If you make a complaint you are confident that it will be dealt with by a manager whose customer satisfaction record is constantly monitored. Everything is geared up to giving the customer 100% service with the premier brand he or she purchased. The price is public knowledge, published and transparent with other leading brands like *BMW* and *Lexus* keeping the price in check. *Mercedes* at the top spot still care because the free market makes them.

Unfortunately, buying accountancy advice does not follow the same pattern. You have to sign a formal legal letter giving the accountants all sorts of get-outs. You are rarely asked for your feedback. You are lucky if you get the feeling they really care about you. If you complain, you are likely to hear 'This is the way we do it'. You could then be jettisoned as a client or put on the back burner.

But you are stuck with this system, which you have to use because most people in business have to have an accountant.

A famous comedian and actor – a prestige client for any – was represented by one of the Big Four accountancy firms. They assigned one or two partners to him and a team of managers to deal with all his affairs, but nobody really got to know him. He got fed up with being passed around from one person to another and not building up a relationship with any of them, so he changed to a chartered accountant, working as a sole practitioner in London, where he became that firm's biggest client. That practitioner got to know the comedian's affairs inside out, calling in specialist expertise when needed. The comedian then moved to a haven in the sun with all the added tax complications and the sole practitioner handled the move and all the overseas matters. Our comedian did not need a string of overseas tax advisors; he just needed one, dedicated, highly qualified professional accountant with good all-round knowledge of his individual case – and that is what he got. He was now getting the right advice. The Big Four brand had not satisfied him despite them charging the highest possible prices.

You get what you pay for - **had not worked**

PRICE

The price is even more of a joke. It is variable under the accountant's control and open to their whim. Fixed prices combat this but are not yet common practice. Charge-out rates are not up front on the websites of those known as the 'Big Four' (*PwC, Ernst & Young, Deloitte & Touche* and *KPMG* – more of which later) or indeed on those of most other chartered accountants, leaving comparisons in a vacuum.

In my later chapter on overcharging, I set out the farcical set of emails that ensued when I tried to get a simple quote from one of the Big Four accountants for my fictitious one-man business. If a scruffy teenager went into a *Mercedes* dealer and said 'I want an economical runner', the dealer might tell him that the insurance could cost as much as the car and he might he be better looking at a *Ford* dealer. Good advice. When I approached one of the big boys they did not at any point tell me that I might be better with a smaller firm of chartered accountants. No, they just carried on through email after email, one department after another, and eventually gave me a quote eight times what I would pay to a small firm. Bad advice or legalised robbery?

As auditors of public companies, the large firms' duty is to report to the shareholders. However, they are effectively appointed by the directors. There are publicised cases of when audit work has been compromised and this often boils down to the influence of the directors. If you are a small fish there will be no compromise. You have zero influence. It will be take it or leave it. This attitude filters downwards through the sizes of firm.

WHERE ARE THEY?

So accountants are all out there feathering their own nests at their clients' expense? But surely amongst the thousands of those bean-counters there must be some who will give good service and advice?

Can you name a famous good accountant? You can name good actors, musicians, politicians, writers. You can name good brands for most types of goods and services – clothes, retailers, supermarkets, mobiles, banks and so on – but can you name a good accountancy 'brand' or company?

The Big Four get championed basically because they are big. There are no surveys, no market appraisals. The internet will make various claims, which we analyse later. Apart from the occasional glib reference in the press, it is all a bit of a mystery. As we have said, *PwC* get generally described as 'top accountants' but many would question their reputation following *Margaret Hodge's* comments in Parliament that *PwC* 'peddle tax avoidance on an industrial scale'. However, that firm is still booming, turning over billions.

I'VE GOT A GOOD ACCOUNTANT

The quality of the average 'high street' firm is judged subjectively based on a particular client's experience – most will claim that the accountancy firm they are using is good because to say they are not up to scratch implies they (the client) are stupid for sticking with them.

Positive affirmations enhance that belief. Taking this a stage further the recommendation to a friend, of your good accountant, with subsequent positive feedback, confirms you were right all along, so your confidence builds in your guy along with your own self-esteem. Nothing really to do with his work, it's all just smoke and mirrors.

Former accountants will be labelled as 'useless' by their ex-clients, some of whom will even use a former accountant as an excuse for their own business failure.

A famous football manager who was acquitted of tax evasion after a high-profile trial said in his defence: 'I got myself a good accountant.' His good accountant was, in fact, a ten-partner London firm that acted for others in his industry.

Did that make them good? He certainly thought so. There are plenty of other firms with a similar number of partners in London; why was this particular outfit described as 'good'? Did he mean they were 'qualified and regulated'? I doubt if he gave it that much thought. Did he mean they acted for some other 'big names'? Yes, probably.

If the jury had found him guilty and he had gone to jail as a public example, how 'good' would his accountant's advice have been then? How 'good' a firm would they then be with one of their prestige clients banged up for tax evasion?

Just imagine if, over lunch with his accountant, he had raised the fact that he was getting a cash payment (or 'bung' as the red tops liked to call it). The partner might have said: 'Well, off the record, if you put it in an overseas account, don't tell me or my staff. Don't put in your own name. It will then be off the radar – just make sure you spend it overseas.'

Or he might have said, 'You should declare everything, it's all taxable', and launched into the dangers of money laundering and tax evasion. The right advice would have been:

> *You are a public figure. HMRC will have you in their spotlight. Declare **all** your earnings or move overseas*

BLIND FAITH

Many people think that once they engage a (recommended) accountant and commit to paying serious fees, their job is done. They have locked on to this professional and therefore discharged their responsibility, they feel that their tax and financial affairs will now be sorted. They, just have to follow what they are told and great advice, service and tax savings will follow automatically. It will cost a bit, but they have done their job. They have found 'financial faith'.

So naturally they think they can now leave it up to him (or her) and concentrate on other things. The accountant will deal with all that area of 'finance'. He will be there when needed. He will anticipate everything. He will advise. Some clients think they can stop altogether. I had one very small delightful client who would never open a brown envelope or one from a bank. She just passed them on to me unopened at the year end with tales of her financial problems. She has now partnered up with someone very rich so her problems got solved.

Unfortunately, the world is littered with many clients who have not received what they expected and have been led over a cliff. They have had bad advice and service, and been overcharged. Some will have changed accountants, others will have stayed with the devil they know, and many will actually be ignorant of whether they are getting good, bad, inadequate or just plain wrong advice, or even whether they are being overcharged.

Imagine that, after you got married, you assumed you were now set up for life. Your job is done; you have found Miss or Mr Right and all will end happily ever after. But any relationship has to be nurtured, and whether it's a personal or a professional relationship, you need to learn to create the right conditions with your accountant, to allow it to flourish.

So where does that leave you? What can you do about it? Well I am going to explain that by using your accountant in an effective way you stand a good chance of moulding him into that good one you want. That it is your attitude and approach to your accountant that can dictate the quality of the advice you get, the service you experience and the charges made on you. He will react to you because his job is basically reactionary. While there may be common standards of service and ethical codes of practice laid down by various bodies, there is still flexibility – quite a lot in fact.

HOW TO JUDGE?

How can you judge what advice you should be getting from your advisor? How can you judge how much tax you should pay? With the absence of independent yardsticks or alternative calculations of your accounts and tax you are pretty stuffed. You fall back on judgements on the coffee, the pleasant receptionist, his smart suit or his manner. These are working away subliminally on your view as you have little else to go on.

This book should give you some knowledge that will move you up the scale so you can judge your position more effectively. You will soon be better-equipped to judge and get the best out of your accountant or, if all fails, to find a new one.

GET THE BEST

There are essentially two stages to follow:

1. First, you need to have the **right type** of accountant acting for you. Accountants vary enormously: there are big firms, small firms, qualified and unqualified accountants, cheap, reasonable and expensive accountants. You have to find the one that suits you or your business.
2. Second, you have to provide the **right conditions** to enable your chosen advisor to give you that good advice, service and fair fees. You might like to think that because you have chosen a good firm then good advice will follow. Well, it might – but just as easily it might not if you make too many mistakes.

DEFINITIONS WE WILL USE

Throughout this book I refer at times to two concepts which impact on accountancy services:

Favoured client

This is what you are aiming to become with your accountant. A build-up of your actions with consistency, so much that your name becomes synonymous with the clients he wants to work for. He will be watching your back like his own. You will be part of his inner circle. You don't have to socialise, in fact, that is discouraged. No, you should aim to be the client he is happy to take calls from even on his mobile. You will be the grateful recipient of those extra tips that are going to save you tax and make things go smoothly, all for a fair and reasonable fee.

Standard professional coverage

This is a term I have coined for what accountants will do for a run-of-the-mill client: that is, the 'textbook advice' or 'bog standard' I referred to before. We will see examples of how this advice can work against you and how a more practical-based approach to your situation can save you thousands. The advice, though, will be technically correct, pretty well unchallengeable, carefully researched and safe. There will be no chance of professional comeback, no sailing close to the wind, just the minimum necessary to keep that client in undisputed legal compliance.

The accountant, or manager if a bigger firm, will go home and sleep soundly or be happy that his superior cannot fault his actions. It will keep you on the straight and narrow, sure, and will cost you a fair bit in fees and maybe in tax.

GET STARTED

If you are happy with **standard professional coverage** then fine, but I suspect most of you will want that little bit more.

So how do you get your advisor to start treating you as one of his **favoured clients**?

By the end of this book you should have a pretty good idea.

2

THE WILD WEST

It's a mess. The accountancy profession is a baffling jungle of different types of firms.

There are multinational corporate firms with thousands of partners, there are single practitioners operating from their kitchen table, and the whole range of companies in between the two, not to mention a kaleidoscope of 'accountancy qualifications' and associations – no wonder the public is confused.

Financial security and independence are vital for your well-being, right up there with satisfactory relationships and good health.

To get you in shape you want a properly trained, qualified, regulated, up-to-date professional handling your affairs and advising you.

Consider the following advert:

This appeared in Accountancy, which was for years the official magazine of the UK Chartered Accountants till they sold and lost control of the content:

Note the last sentence, which I have underlined. You need **no background in accountancy** to start up. So how do you know whether your 'accountant' is up to the job or dealing with your finances properly to get the best results? The truth is, you don't.

A large nationwide franchise was claiming that your affairs were in the 'safe hands of experts'. An easy claim to make in the unregulated system that is in place. But are they really experts? Not necessarily.

Contrast this: the training period before setting up on your own to do small-business end of year tax returns and accounts is:

> The franchise......................six weeks
>
> Chartered accountants.......five years

The difference is monumental. **Are chartered accountants dumb or is someone being conned?**

Anyone who has a persuasive manner and can more or less get the accounts out could be in business. Any Tom, Dick or

Harry can be out there set up as a practising 'accountant'. No experience or qualifications necessary.

Your financial affairs can be as important to you as your health, yet your advisors can be authorised quacks. They can be out there charging you £500 for a job which takes them an hour and which they are not trained properly to do. This is going on **now**.

HOW ARE THEY GETTING AWAY WITH IT?

On the whole, if you go to a solicitor he or she has to be regulated by the *Law Society* and to hold a practising certificate, which in turn requires them to have liability insurance as a protection for clients if anything goes wrong. Nobody can just call themselves a solicitor and so the public usually have confidence that their legal advisor is at least properly qualified. They happily hand over large amounts of money without really checking up on the firm or the partners.

If someone, say, does a bit of bookkeeping for a local builder they may well decide to call themselves an accountant. They can set up websites, join networks and procure clients. They can even set up a brass plaque such as:

Smith Jones & Co. Accountants and Tax Advisors

And they don't even have to be called Smith or Jones! When I set up in practice in 1982 the name of the accountancy firm had to be based on partners or former partners.

On top of letting all these cowboys open up shop the regulators/government have given them a playing field steeply sloped in their favour.

ALPHABET SOUP

Okay but they have got letters after their name, they must be qualified. Oh no, another joke?

A friend of mine was given a Lordship as a present. He does not use it except in banter but the point is it was bought. You can also buy your way into 'accountancy' letters with some lip service to unofficial bodies that just seem to spring up out of nowhere.

I do not know what all these accountants' letters stand for. How the hell are the public supposed to?

ACA, FCA, ACCA, FCCA, CA, ACMA, FCMA, CPFA, AAIA, FAIA, AAPA, FFA, AFA, ACPA, FCPA, ICPA, MAAT, FMAAT, AIAB, FIAB, AFT... and more!

The first four in bold are those of the main UK bodies for regulated accountants. The supervising bodies of these first four are the *Institute of Chartered Accountants* and the *Chartered Association of Certified Accountants*. The addition of the F (Associate to Fellow) in the letters signifies extra experience garnered through more years in practice. The 'F' letter seemed like a good idea in archaic times, but it just confuses the public now and should be scrapped. Yawn. The rest of the qualifications listed are various associations that have set up on the back of the main bodies; because they can in our crazy system.

Example

There is (or was) a body called *The Association of Tax Agents* and their website said:

If you claim a tax refund, be sure to use a company bonded by the Association of Tax Agents (ATA). If a company is not bonded by the ATA and goes out of business, you could lose your refund.'

97% of travellers who work in the UK overpay their PAYE tax. However, the Inland Revenue laws allow this overpayment to be repaid to the taxpayer. A large number of tax agents have sprung up, offering to act on the behalf of the taxpayer in claiming this money back. They normally charge a commission rate (between 15% and 25%) on the amount received.

In the past 4 years, several tax agents in the UK have gone out of business. These insolvencies were caused by one of two reasons:

An intent to defraud their clients, by keeping the tax rebate, not paying the money over to the client and closing the business.

Charging unusually low commission rates, in a bid to generate more business. This causes the company to lose money and to face closure, and spend the client's funds to cover operating costs.

The Association of Tax Agents was formed in 1998 to protect the clients of member companies against financial loss. To become a member of the ATA, the companies have to satisfy strict entry criteria, in particular, maintaining a separate client account for monies collected from Inland Revenue.

Since the ATA was formed, no bonded member has ceased trading. However, in the unlikely event of a company facing closure, the ATA will take over the processing of the refund application when the Inland Revenue has not yet paid out the rebate. You will not be charged any more than was previously agreed with by *the original Tax Agent Company. In the situation whereby the Inland Revenue has already paid out on a claim and the Tax Agent Company has received the rebate, the ATA does not have any liability. The ATA is not responsible for another member company's action in this situation. If this is the case, the ATA will contact the Inland Revenue and determine the details of the payment.*

If you require more information please email: info@associationoftaxagents.co.uk

There are two issues here which should ring alarm bells:

1. The least you should expect is that your accountant is up to date. In the 2004 Budget – yes, over a decade ago – the name Inland Revenue was changed to HM Revenue and Customs and officially implemented in 2005. Still, some 12 years, later this 'accountancy' organisation refers to it by its old name.
2. As of January 2016 their website listed they only had six members servicing the small business sector , whereas the *Institute of Chartered Accountants* has some 20,000.

HIGH STREETS

So we have a medley of confusing letters, professional labels and professional bodies. Can it get worse? Oh yes, because the qualified guys hide themselves away on the first floor of a building while the 'quacks' are better at getting the shop-front positions and the highest positions on *Google*.

In your local high street the most high-profile accountancy business is likely to be a non-qualified practice. Your qualified guy may display a small brass plate or letters on a window somewhere, but the non-qualified practitioner will be better at catching the public eye.

So our small business, individual or sub-contractor is first attracted to these firms and often engages them by convenience.

REGISTERED WITH HMRC?

If you *Google* 'tax refunds' you will be offered numerous firms who purport to offer this service. Many operate outside the regulatory system, with HMRC allowing them to register as an agent with no background check.

Noddy could register as your HMRC agent. It appears that *Noddy* did - have a look at this complaint I found on the internet:

To whom it may concern

Having returned to my home country of South Africa for holiday, I am extremely disappointed concerning my tax return. I want to open a police case against JOHN VERDI TAX REFUNDS LTD for fraudulent activity.

A brief description of the situation is as follows:

I used the above agent/company to file my tax return for the year of 2008/09.

I also indirectly gave Her Majesty's Revenue and Customs the authority to credit my tax return of £3660 to the account of the above mentioned. JOHN VERDI was then meant to credit my account with the amount of £3575 having deducted an £85 fixed service charge.

My online account at HMRC states that the tax refund was issued on the 17th of MAY 2009 and this was credited to my online account. This was then credited to JOHN VERDI's account.

I then waited for 2 weeks but the funds were still not transferred to my account.

I then contacted JOHN VERDI the week beginning the 1st of JUNE 2009 and I spoke to an agent called Martin Simmons. He mentioned to me that they have changed their payment structure and cannot transfer the funds electronically and that they would now be operating a cheque only payment method. Although, Martin Simmons said that because I am in South Africa, they could make an exception and electronically transfer the funds to my Barclays account. However, he would need to confirm this. I then rang Martin Simmons on Thursday the 4th of June and he confirmed that the transfer would be made the following week.

The following Wednesday I tried to contact Martin Simmons but was unsuccessful as the call was directed to the answer phone. The answer phone message stated that John Verdi Tax Consultancy would be unavailable for a short period of time as they were moving premises from Woodford, London to Newcastle. The message also conveyed that if more information was required customers could visit their website.

Having browsed their website I noticed that under the UPDATE section it stated that they will be unavailable for a period of between 2 to 6 weeks.

I continued to visit their website frequently and on the 15 of JULY 2009 their website was removed from the internet, loading a UKREG page mentioning that they have reserved their host name of; JOHNVERDITAXREFUNDS.COM.

I have contact the Companies House and this agent isn't even listed under a registered LTD.

I have not heard anything from them since.

Regards

This would not happen if the system was properly regulated. No properly qualified accountant who has undergone years of training, sweated through exam after exam to get his certificate, is going to run off with £3,000.

THE NON-PAYMENT EFFECT

Let's have a look at an example of what happens at the lower end of the scale of accountancy services.

Someone, say a plumber, has a number of PAYE jobs over the year and is deducted tax (emergency tax) on each one. He also works for a builder and gets deducted SC60 tax. He has earned about £12,000 over the year and has had about £2,000 deducted in tax. He is confused by the system, has no idea what to do, but feels he should not be paying this amount of tax on such small earnings. He has debts, is in arrears with his rent and really needs that £2,000 back. He goes into a shop advertising:

> **Accountants – tax refunds here, no up-front costs**

The friendly person in the shop tells him they can calculate his correct tax, complete all the forms and get his refund. They will only charge if he gets a repayment. This sounds just what he needs and, he thinks, what could be fairer? He has to sign quite a few forms and come back the next day with his passport and utility bill. He leaves all his papers containing details of his income and deductions with the accountant, looking forward to his windfall.

When he leaves, the accountant enters all his income and deductions on a computer program which takes him about 10 minutes. The tax return is then done and at the push of a button is submitted. The accountant then sits back and waits for the refund to pop into his bank account.

For this service will our plumber be charged fairly? Say his tax refund is £2,900. The firm will charge him 20% of that, so he will be charged £580. This, plus VAT, will be deducted from his refund and he will get a check for the balance of £2,204. This is the most he has ever had in a single cheque, he can pay his debts off and he is over the moon. He then goes down the pub to celebrate, telling his mates what a great accountant he has.

This system relies on what I call the non-payment effect. When you get a service and you do not physically have to pay out, it always seems better 'value'. The financial services industry used to be awash with these hidden charges leaving most none the wiser. So our plumber is not minded to complain and he has no inkling that he has paid an unqualified accountant the equivalent rate of about £1,160 per hour.

You might say, well they have overheads of a shop front, in a high street, rates are expensive. Okay, but a big reason they have the shop front is to attract these undiscerning passers-by and add an aura of respectability. You could do the work from your spare room.

THE CLIENT ACCOUNT

Something that purports to add respectability may not be all that it seems.

Client accounts are used by solicitors and chartered accountants. There are strict rules governing the operation of these accounts. Those rules:

- Prevent you from transferring money about willy-nilly.
- Require inspection of all the entries twice a year.
- Require you to wait 30 days after sending your fee bill to client before transferring the money.
- Require you to get a letter from the bank confirming that the designated 'client account' is completely separate from the firm's other accounts and could not in the event of an insolvency be incorporated in the firm's funds.

Unqualified accountants, who are not subject to such rules, can open up an ordinary bank account and call it a client account but it is actually their own bank account in every sense, just with a different name. They have no rules to comply with. It gives no additional protection because without the specific designation it would be classed as part of the company's assets and not the client's.

So, as we see, the system is open to all sorts of abuse. Surprise, surprise.

WHY ARE WE IN THIS SITUATION?

The government and the chartered accountants' organisation have just let this happen. Why? The answer is mainly that the overseeing body of chartered accountants is dominated by the boys from the big firms. Their concern is *big* audits and *big* fees for spin-offs. Small firms have been shouting about it for years but these *big* boys, with deaf ears, controlling the organisation, have marginalised the needs of the thousands of smaller practices serving the majority of UK businesses.

The non-qualified entrepreneurs, sensing an inroad, have marched onto the territory inhabited by sleepwalking, regulated, small-firm chartered accountants, scooping the business from under their noses. While competition is a good thing, it is not so good on a bumpy playing field – and not when it is detrimental to the consumer. This unfair competition is now endemic in the whole system of accountancy services for the small business sector in the UK.

Some unqualified practitioners, however, have got it right, provided a good service and ended up as multimillionaires. *Simon Dolan* set up *SJD Accountancy* in 1992 and then became the largest sole practitioner in the UK. It was recently sold in a £100 million deal.

His autobiography is aptly called *How to make millions without a degree'*. I would have liked *How to whip millions from under chartered accountants' noses.*

CAN WE LEARN LESSONS?

We certainly can. Other countries have regulated their accountants in practice effectively. In the US you are either a CPA (certified public accountant) or not. The letters have statutory protection and if you are qualified (by exams) but have not kept up the ongoing training you have to use 'CPA inactive'. People just say 'go and see a CPA'. Although there are differences state to state in the US, and lower-tier qualifications, 'certified' is the key word that everybody can understand.

Texas has gone further and made the word 'accountant' protected by law.

UK solicitors now have to put 'non-practising' after their fully won qualification 'solicitor' so that there is no confusion for the public.

When it comes to accountants over here we are vague with the **get yourself a good accountant**. This phrase is often used and the ambiguous word 'good' in this context makes up for the lack of a proper title.

DRACONIAN RULES

We hear about accountancy scandals and mistakes. The *Enron* one in the US, for example, and closer to home the recent, but fairly light, *Tesco* debacle. At the end of the next chapter we summarise some of the accounting scandals from *Wikipedia* so the scale can be seen. They generally involve the Big Four firms. When there is a scandal then new regulation on accountants can follow as a reaction. The trouble is that regulation has a catch-all effect on the smaller members of the *Institute of Chartered Accountants*, hitting those 20,000 small-firm members in practice.

This is a heavy burden on the tens of thousands of small practices throughout the country. As we know, regulation has grown in all areas of business, and chartered accountants are no exception. For members to keep their coveted chartered accountant status they have to abide by rules and regulations and suffer extra costs, of course; while their 'high street' unregulated competitors do not. The extra costs for these are not insignificant:

- Professional indemnity insurance, which a small practice could pay between £2,000 and £10,000 for. Premiums are set by reference to the general market, meaning the small accountants are effectively paying for the big firms' mistakes.
- The requirement for continuing professional development (CPD). Regulated accountants have to pay to subscribe to professional educational providers and do the required number of hours 'learning' per year.
- On top of these are the membership and practising fees – in the region of £1,000 per year.
- The dreaded audit and monitoring that chartered accountants are subjected to, where 'inspectors' comb your premises searching for miniscule errors

to justify their existence as 'police' for the institute. They will pick up on trivialities like an undated telephone call note, or a passport that was copied but did not have 'confirmation' written on it. These inspections are costly, stressful and unnecessary experiences, especially for a sole practitioner who is dealing with everything on his or her own.

WHAT YOU GET

The difference between the regulated and unregulated accountants is vast. Look at this:

<u>Regulated and unregulated</u>

- ✓ Can do tax returns and accounts
- ✓ Have to be regulated for money laundering

<u>Regulated only</u>

- ✓ Can carry out audits
- ✓ Have to keep up to date on tax and law changes
- ✓ Are regulated by rules of conduct
- ✓ You can complain and get their work investigated
- ✓ Are subject to heavy penalties for breaches of regulations
- ✓ Files inspected and checked randomly
- ✓ Have to keep your files for proper lengths of time
- ✓ Have to hand over all files on transfer to another accountant
- ✓ Have had to pass very hard exams
- ✓ Have had to do long training and practice work
- ✓ Have to pay professional body fees
- ✓ Have to have insurance

From this, it seems obvious that paying that bit more for a regulated accountant will get you better service – although 'that bit more' can vary from a little to a whole lot more, as I explain in Chapter 7 and 8.

WHY SHOULD THEY BOTHER BEING REGULATED?

You can see why businesses would choose to trade in the 'free-for-all market' as unqualified and unregulated.

There is no financial comeback on these unregulated firms. They are not overseen by the *Financial Conduct Agency* or *Bank of England*, nor is there a professional body or ombudsman to contact who can investigate and fine them. In fact, if things go wrong (assuming you become aware of it), you are stuffed.

They are, however, subject to money laundering regulations, which basically just entails them asking for a passport or utility bill and reporting fraudsters. Funny how this can actually add respectability. When they ask for ID documents, just like banks, solicitors etc., then clients think these guys must be properly regulated. Far from it – the money laundering requirements have nothing to do with the service you will get. Unregulated firms are inspected by HMRC in relation to their money laundering. All they have to do is get that ID info on a file, assess how risky you are and occasionally check your ID status. Then, if you evade tax, they are under a duty to report you. Unregulated firms are free to exaggerate or rip you off as much as their own natural desire for money will allow without comeback.

Unfortunately, this system of the unregulated operating in the regulated sector has been allowed to develop over the years to such an extent that it will take a major disaster – perhaps like the one that hit the banking world – before the authorities will react. The trouble is, this is unlikely to happen. These unregulated accountants service small, non-related businesses, so the odd SME (small and medium-sized enterprises) disaster will have little general impact and confine itself to that small business. It is not going to surface like the mis-selling scandals, it just lurks there undetectably. Clients put their problems down to their own bad choice and move on.

It's too late to make the word 'accountant' protected in the UK so the answer is for the certified association to merge with the chartered accountants, drop all the letters and just become a CA or chartered accountant. Keep it simple. Then let the public know the facts by an advertising campaign. Also apply 'light touch' regulation to the small practitioners who are having to compete with the unregulated, going some way to levelling the playing field.

We led the world for centuries in the field of accountancy, with many emerging countries copying and adopting our system.

We now lead the world in confusion.

3

CHARTERED

Chartered Accountants were the original 'brand' launched in 1894 in Britain. The name 'chartered' expanded throughout the Commonwealth and is still considered the premier brand in most English-speaking countries, although not generally adopted in the EU.

The *Institute of Chartered Accountants in England and Wales* (ICAEW) has over the years run marketing campaigns promoting the value of using their member firms who, they claim, stand out from others in the field who may be unqualified. Have you seen this promotion? Unlikely. As we have seen, the ICAEW is not masterly in promoting the interests of its members.

The ICAEW is a self-regulating body. To retain this status it has to show that it has standards and maintains them by enforcement. We have seen how this skews the market in the 'Wild West'. They also make it hard to qualify with training and exams where many fall by the wayside. So, prima face, standards are high and kept in check.

Because the brand conveys quality, others want to jump on its bandwagon and have indeed managed to do so, taking advantage of the confusing system.

The separate body of accountants for years called 'certified accountants', denoted by the letters ACCA, has usurped the name chartered. They lobbied to get the word chartered inserted in their title. In 1971 they changed their name to the *Association of Certified Accountants*. In 1984 they changed it to the *Chartered Association of Certified Accountants* and later, in 1996, they changed it to the *Association of Chartered Certified Accountants*. By the backdoor they attained the status of chartered accountants in the eyes of the public without having to go through what is generally regarded as tougher training

The 'chartered' brand experiences some fees resistance but does not put off many businesses and individuals who would not consider employing anyone other than a chartered accountant to look after their affairs. They are prepared to – and most can – pay for quality. The directors of many *FTSE* and successful companies are chartered accountants and this helps the brand to retain its credibility, not just in the UK but worldwide.

CODE OF ETHICS

Inherent in the chartered accountants' brand is their code of ethics. The profession make much play out of this so it's probably worth setting out what is claimed. If you want chapter and verse, look on the ICAEW website. They maintain it is fundamental to promoting trust and inspiring confidence. So what do they claim?

They say they will:

- be straightforward and honest
- make sure actions will reflect words
- be open to suggestions
- correct mistakes
- consider the public interest
- not mislead

Pretty fine words which should apply to any business. But note there is no reference to charging a fair price. The implication is you can charge what you can get away with as long as you stick to a few basic rules. That makes the profession pretty happy with the directive, but not so the public. Unfortunately, these 'ethical' accountants inhabit a world where getting away with bumping up fees is all too easy.

Also, every one of those six ethical mantras can be 'covered up' fairly cleverly to the untrained, uninformed public.

You may be better protected in the regulated sector but I am not saying you are off the hook.

FOUR TYPES OF CHARTERED FIRMS

More confusion stems from the fact that 'chartered accountants' embraces four different types of firms:

1. The Big Four – *PwC, Deloitte, KPMG, Ernst &Young*
2. The next 50
3. Medium (provincial) firms
4. Small firms.

There are distinctions between them and how they service clients.

The Big Four

London-led, all these have more than 500 'partners' and are huge companies who, by being legally charged as the auditors of FTSE companies, spin off into the whole range of financial services. They charge massive fees, making their partners multimillionaires with relatively little risk.

Size and the brand here are everything. That Big Four name on your annual audit report gives credibility (banks and others can be easily impressed). They are your auditors, implying respectability, objective ability and profitability.

That objectivity may well hold for the most but there are many cases of compromise and conflict of interest when big clients, big fees and big personalities have dominated and the interests of the shareholders they are supposed to protect have been sidelined.

So, if you have four firms all doing pretty much the same thing at the same price, how do you choose? You may have tenders, slick presentations from partners who excel in selling, but an easy audit ride, tax and consultancy skills can win the day.

The *Royal Bank of Scotland's* infamous *Mr Goodwin* became chief executive following a career as a chartered accountant. Auditing a huge bank, as RBS was, and the rapid growth it undertook, is an expensive, complex and skilled job involving hundreds of professionals. One of his first actions was to sack the current auditors, who knew the systems well, and replace them with the firm where he had begun his career.

For a FTSE financial director who does not really care about the size of the audit fee, any Big Four name will be okay for his other directors and the shareholders. So, if his old pal from accountancy college is the audit partner of a Big Four firm, it's a no-brainer. He may have an audit committee to officially ratify the appointment but are they going to upset the FD?

Big Four firms have top tax specialists who can be paid five times the salary of an HMRC inspector to provide 'extras' to their audit clients. They exploit every tax loophole and haven going, complying, of course, to the letter with UK and international tax legislation. These firms have been accused of encouraging tax avoidance/evasion but are, after all, only responding to the demands of their clients for these extra services.

For commercial organisations, tax is just another expense and these back-room boys are there helping push profits up by devising schemes and loopholes allowed in our democratic, capitalist free-market economy. They aid in the quest for higher profits and so better shareholder returns. It is results-driven, so commands top fees authorised by back-patted directors who don't have to pay them out of their own pockets.

A Big Four firm devised a complicated tax scheme for an international brewing company to avoid millions in tax; they also just happened to be their auditors. In the ensuing challenges the brewers proffered the usual excuse of 'we pay lots of PAYE and VAT'. That may be true but paying over PAYE and VAT is just a tax collection exercise – it is not their own tax and does not affect their profit.

Companies and people need to run their businesses effectively which in turn means keeping their tax as low as possible. The tax system is so complicated that if you are not effective in this direction you can pay more tax than you should. If the public wants fairer tax payments, then Parliament must change the laws.

While small businesses are generally better served by the medium and small accountancy firms, these Big Four do not turn them away. Some offer remote services for small businesses and will, if approached, take them on as clients. Just watch out on fees if you stray off the remote bundle.

The next 50

These are the larger chartered accountancy practices that essentially serve the companies and businesses which are below the listed companies but still require complex accountancy and tax advice and statutory audits. They also look after high net worth clients, smaller businesses and specialist occupations. These firms can still charge fees that make people gulp. They are generally not suitable for small and medium-sized enterprises (SMEs) looking for an economical service. Many will claim they do have small business departments specifically for SMEs, and these indeed could appear competitive. They provide the service to a **standard professional coverage** level but their charges will generally be higher than the medium or smaller regulated firms providing an equally good service and maybe going an extra mile or two as well.

You may find that the staff change frequently in these firms, especially as you will get assigned 'trainees' who naturally move around a lot. A partner may head it up but will tend to only get involved with the larger paying clients. His charge-out rate may prohibit any dealings with small paying clients.

Having the same people deal with your affairs year on year has advantages. A fellow accountant was managing director (MD) of a large charity who used a Top 50 firm to audit the foundation. The audit took about four days and each year two new members of staff from that audit firm would come to the premises to do the audit. The first day of the audit would be spent with the MD explaining the systems to them, as he did in previous years to the previous auditors. He was of course charged for all the time it took re-teaching the systems to the two new staff. The partner in the accountancy firm had no real involvement in the job apart from effectively taking the profit; probably about 50% of the fee. Being a well-financed charitable foundation, whose remit was just to give away its income after expenses each year, there was no commercial need to keep a check on costs to the extent that it was necessary to 'shop around'.

The medium brand

The 'medium' brand refers to firms of, say, between four and ten partners often sited in provincial towns. They will have nice offices, staffing of anything from ten to fifty and generate a feeling of efficiency and competence. So what is the advantage of this sort of firm? Continuity, reliability, resources, its competent professional advice and the general local standing can be impressive.

The partners may all live fairly locally and each have their own circle of contacts, networks and bank of clients. They will deal with local banks and financial advisors. A chartered firm of that size will take great care with HMRC compliance and professional regulations. Their output to clients should be first class and PR driven. Nice reception, local sponsorship, press releases and a generally smart appearance. All in all, that leads to a good reputation of professionalism going round and round in the locality. If the partners have good personal skills and know their stuff, their brand will flourish in their area and wider through their sphere of contacts.

The disadvantages, perhaps, are firstly, that they will have to keep up standards and recruit the best staff they can get and prices will have to reflect this. This in turn will push their charges up above a small, two-partner-type firm. PAs, larger overheads and the PR and HR departments all get costed in, creating the need for higher fees.

Secondly, the advice will be sanitised and staff-led, falling to the **standard professional coverage** mentioned earlier. But the recommendations, the developed brand and standing will give confidence to clients who, not knowing other accountants, will entrust their affairs to the care of these bigger practices, feeling that they will be getting the best advice. This is reinforced by paying handsomely for it.

Having paid to go with this established firm and its staff, you can still create your own personal rapport with your partner and the tips through this book should aid in that. The partner does not have to do all the routine accounts work himself but, to deal effectively with your affairs, he needs to know your individual circumstances and have a review meeting with you from time to time to finalise detailed points, so that he can give you advice that will save you money.

So, these medium firms have a brand and they will undoubtedly claim to have this 'good reputation' – not just with (new) clients but with associated professionals, like bank managers, solicitors and financial planners, who are no doubt on favourable terms and are their chief sources of recommendation.

Existing clients will always praise their current guys, but what about a survey of ex-clients? That's never done, of course. Every firm will have ex-clients who think they were treated badly, given bad advice or overcharged. But you will never hear from them. Some firms have more skeletons than others, but these stay safely locked in the cupboard because generally ex-clients have no connection with each other, so their opinions are never shared.

Such firms can either just remain with the one main office, doing what they do, making good profits, or they can expand and grow. They could even be an aggressive take-over operation, building up their fees by acquiring small practices to become one of the Top 50 (in size) accountants. One accountancy practice did this and is now a national firm built up by acquisition of small ones.

Small firms

Alongside the 20,000 firms of *chartered* accountants in the UK there are also many members of the more international body of *certified* accountants. These two organisations make up the bulk of the small firms throughout the UK. They are small-business specialists. In every small town you will find at least one practice and often several in larger towns.

They are very much led by the partners' rapport with existing clients, and their personal contacts.

The firms will have a local presence and most clients will come in through some form of recommendation or personal contact. Internet and advertising usually pay only a small part. The firms rely on the partners to build relations with associates, clients, business networks etc. They build the firm's client bank; as some clients will naturally drop off so new ones continually need to be found.

In fact, new clients for these firms can come from anywhere. On holiday I once went to a specialist shop to buy a windsurfing sailboard. I did not get the sailboard that day but came out with the shop as a client. How? He asked me what I did and I said I was an accountant; he said he was not happy with his, so we started talking and one thing led to another.

A regulated small firm could be just a 'sole practitioner', that is a person on his or her own, maybe with a few staff. This can have its disadvantages. The practitioner can get ill, have a life change or suddenly sell out. You can get over this by choosing a firm with at least two partners. Having said that, regulated sole accountants are required to have procedures in place to guard against retirement, so if your sole accountant is chartered you have that protection. Your files and affairs are probably quite safe in the event of the practitioner's demise, as you would most likely find another qualified accountant taking over the practice quickly with access to your files. Practices are bought and sold for a figure of about 1.25 times your fee aggregated with all the other fees. Support staff would probably stay on and your affairs should not suffer.

It is good to find a firm that has been around for some time and has built up its clients by recommendation. This should indicate they care for their clients and their reputation.

They should have a broad range of clients, too. If they are regulated, fully computerised, have a good website and appear modern and up to date in their approach, then they are ahead of the game and the outlook is pretty promising.

This type of small firm does offer better continuity. The support staff generally stay longer and a business client can benefit from less disruption if they have the same audit or accounts partner and staff that know their business year on year. While a new team can pick up things previously missed, generally you are better served by continuity.

Besides the professional labelling, the sole practitioner or small firm will have a form of 'individual' branding in their locality. That is, the brand of the partner himself. Many sole practitioners and small-firm partners take great pains to establish their own particular brand. They can hook on to a niche, a specialism, or just solid work at fair prices. They get known locally by serving clients and building up trust. They are convenient and usually reasonably priced. Their personality is important, combining the attributes of a salesmen and a technician, often in the most subtle of ways. The good ones develop a 'bedside manner' to rival the best doctors', getting their clients to look up to them as a kind of guru who has all the answers to their business issues..

One charismatic practitioner I knew operated in a sleepy country village. He was involved in many local community events. He would talk to everybody, listen to their problems and exude charm. Everyone went to him about their tax and accounts. They loved their chats, getting his views on what they were doing and how they should be going. It got to point where he was personally overloaded and totally stressed. His solution in the end was to double all his fees. Half his clients left in shock but half stayed and he became much happier making the same money for half the time input.

Those that develop their own brand have personality and qualities that inspire confidence and trust. Even in a two-partner firm, the partners will have their own stamp with their personal bank of clients. Partners who have really established their personal brand will tend to have better and bigger clients, which in many cases can lead the firm on to the next stage without actually expanding or being taken over.

BIG FIRM SCANDALS

The big firms have overseen many accounting scandals covering things such as:

> *Business loans, inflated sales, Bernie Madoff's Ponzi scheme, illegal payments, round trip trades, understated earnings, incorrect cost overruns, overstated asset values, misleading accounting practices, disclosure failures, fictitious transactions in Korea, falsified accounting documents and accounts, overstated cash flows.*

Big firms have been responsible for significant accounting errors in some large multinational companies (details are available on *Wikipedia* where the following information was found).

> *Adelphis, Autonomy, Duke Energy, El Paso, Merrill Lynch, Nortel, Reliant Energy, Royal Abold, Unify*

> *AIG, Bristol Myers, Freddie Mac, Kmart, Merck, Micro Strategy, Satyam Computer, Swiss Air, Tyco*

> *Anglo Irish Bank, AOL, Cendal, Chiquita, HeathSouth, Informix, Lehman Bros, Olympus, One. Tel, Simo Forest, Sybase, Toshiba*

> *Computer Associates, In Clone, Kinross, Lermot, Mirant, Peregrine, Xerox*

WHAT'S THE CHARTERED FUTURE?

The big firms are here to stay. Despite the heat of scandals or tax avoidance, they will adapt and prosper. They are endemic in the system with many graduates desperate to become part of them.

It is down the chain where the inherent differences in the system will bring about change. The confusion, the rise of unregulated firms and the disappearing chartered small practitioner will all have an effect.

The high-street unqualified outfits could grow. Small firms of chartered accountants will diminish.

Over the last 30 years or so, many small firms have stopped training students. Entry to the prime professional qualification is now mostly though the Big Four and Top 50 firms' route. New entrants are not being attracted to the small chartered firms.

Businesses could be faced with choosing the unregulated sector for their accountancy services or going to a 'qualified' big firm which will charge a lot more.

Some qualified small chartered accountants are even giving up their hard-won title of 'chartered' so they can continue to practise just as accountants, dropping the 'chartered' to get themselves out of the regulatory regime and those extra costs. They still have the same clients and the local reputation. Clients don't see any difference. The word 'chartered' is irrelevant to existing clients when they know the firm and the brand has become the individual they respect and have confidence in.

4

CHOOSING

If you can find the right service locally, you might well be tempted to choose that one. It can often be cheaper and more efficient. But guess what? You don't really need a local guy. You may only visit your accountant once or twice a year, if at all, so it's not a big deal if you have to travel a bit to see them. If all your accountant does for you is your annual accounts, a lot goes on by email, phone and post. So don't worry if he isn't on the doorstep. Finding the right guy for the job is more important than geographical location.

REMOTE SERVICES

Web-based accountants and some specialist departments of large firms are now offering remote services all over the UK, even within the Big Four. You never meet an accountant face-to-face but you have access by email and phone for all queries. Books and records are sent by post or as computer files. Often they recommend a computer package, such as *Xero*, for you to use. A software package that links into their system has big advantages in getting your data to them.

This process can work well for many clients, but you lose that face-to-face interaction which you get from a personal meeting. We see later how a meeting or a visit to your premises may get you that extra advice or save you money but this is not likely to happen in the standard system where your affairs are sanitised, packaged up and put to bed.

People also like a put a face to their advisor, if only at the start. We have more confidence after a face-to-face, which is especially relevant in something as important as financial affairs. Also, remember that the theme of this book is to get into that **favoured client** position and that is impossible with a remote one. You will by default get the **standard professional coverage.**

Effectively you do not have 'an accountant' you have a **system** presenting itself as 'your accountant'.

RECOMMENDATIONS

Traditionally, this has been regarded as the best way to choose an accountant. Up until about 25 years ago, word-of-mouth was virtually the only means by which accountants could stand on their reputation. It is still probably the most common method of getting an accountant in the regulated sector.

Recommendations can come from virtually anyone. However, you are unlikely to ask a friend who has just gone bankrupt to recommend his accountant. Usually people pick someone they know well or look up to for a recommendation.

People feel that there is nothing quite like a personal recommendation for a good positive start; far better than taking pot luck from the internet or the local paper. When you go as a recommendation you are in a 'one-up' position. Accountants do not want you to go back to your recommender and say 'that guy was awful' or 'he dropped me right in it', so you are already in a superior position and feel comfortable that this person is going to work well for you.

If you have gone on the recommendation of someone highly successful, you may think that person's success is due in part to having the right accountant. You are most likely to be wrong on that count, though – your friend/acquaintance would most likely have been successful whatever accountant he had chosen.

WHO TO ASK?

Asking a professional such as a lawyer, financial advisor or bank manager can seem like a good idea but caution is needed, as you may unknowingly be entering the murky waters of commissions and referrals – in other words, a world of non-objective recommendations. You would be surprised how often there are tie-ups and arrangements between professional firms. Commissions or favours can be exchanged for referrals without you knowing, or a system of cross-referrals operates: one firm may pass on clients and get others in return. Not all do this but some certainly do. It's not all wrong, as many businesses work in this way. However, while it may be acceptable to hire a decorator or builder like this, your accountant is a serious, long-term relationship, so you don't really want to start with one through a backhander as opposed to a genuine recommendation.

Your best bet is probably the lawyer or solicitor. If he's not in anyone's pocket he will probably say he can't recommend anyone, although he knows many. He may temper this and give you a list of, say, three. That's a good sign.

If you are given a list, great – pick the bottom one.

INTERNET

New outfits are springing up where you can find a 'vouched for' professional. Accountants are encouraged to join the recommendation website and get charged a fee for referrals. The website tells the accountants who sign up to get reviews from clients and upload them to the site. Some accountants are getting them in the hundreds. The thing is these are not really 'reviews'. We understand reviews for films or books, indeed, and they are independent views of the product. These purported reviews are far from that. They are just mostly made up promotional pieces. The website says they are 'checked', but all that involves is a confirmation from a different email address. It's funny how 99% of the 'reviews' give the accountant five stars out of five. Take it with a pinch of salt. The system is open to massive abuse.

FEES DISADVANTAGE

Your prospective accountant knows that when people come to him on recommendation there is a 95% certainty that he will secure them as a client. All he has to do is keep up appearances and not make himself look an idiot or create negative rapport at the first meeting. All he wants *you* to do is to want him to act for you so much that when he mentions his charges you dismiss it as 'no problem'. That is his only aim.

Lack of competitiveness on fees can be the main problem with recommendations. When you go on a tip from someone then usually this is known to the accountant and he knows how to maximise *his* benefit from this recommendation. This gives the accountant the upper hand.

One accountancy firm said to me that they had all the clients they want, so when a new client gets recommended they quote very high. If they never hear from them again they don't care and if they become a client, the firm makes a handsome profit. It's a win either way for the firm, but not necessarily for that client.

YOUR MATE HARRY

Jack asks Harry who he uses as his accountant and Harry says 'Mr Smith is great. He has always done my accounts well. He got rid of my tax this year. He seems to know his stuff. He's a good guy.'

Wow, that's a fantastic recommendation. You go and see Harry's accountant, and he's very personable and knows his stuff, just as Harry said. You think: 'This guy's for me. I don't need to see anyone else, he will be great.'

But look more closely. The patter of well-meaning Harry is flawed. Let's look at his statements:

He's great – this means nothing. Who has he got to compare him with – *Monty Python*?

He has always done my accounts well – by what standard? Harry has no way of knowing – what is he comparing the work with –his own disastrous attempts?

He got rid of my tax this year – that was because Harry made less profit than the year before, and his payments on account wiped out this year's tax. Nothing to do with the accountant's work, it's just the rules, yet the accountant gets all the credit.

He seems to know his stuff – the average client does not understand the technical bits (note the word 'seems') and so he appeared to be a genius.

He's a good guy – I didn't get into trouble with the Revenue. And my business still seems to be afloat, therefore he must be good?

On analysis the whole basis for the recommendation is flawed.

However, two things actually flow from a recommendation:

1. Harry has not had problems with the work done
2. A recommendation has a safe ring to it

You are not starting from zero, you are already on the bottom rung of the ladder. The lack of any (known) error speaks for itself and the recommendation has a slight tone of guarantee. The fact that the firm appears flawless and is recommended sets a standard that most will want to maintain. Recommendations are still the best way – if approached with some caution and objective judgement.

Another reason recommendations are beneficial is the 'family effect'. If an accountant has built up his clientele through the recommendations of friends and family, many will know each other. Bad work will be talked about and judgements made, so there is an inbuilt incentive for the accountant to do a good job.

BANK OR FRIEND

But things can go astray. Do you trust the banks? Despite 'bankers backlash', many still respect the advice of their local manager, if you can still find one or get past security.

Let's look at Mr and Mrs Fryer. They run a small but growing catering business. Mrs Fryer used to work for an insurance company and for the first two years had done their own accounts and tax. It was getting too complicated now so they need an accountant.

They had lined up two from recommendations. There was Nigel their local butcher – he said he has used Clot & Co. for years - and Fred Goodman their local bank manager has said Mason, Stone and Partners were 'particularly good'. The Fryers tended to favour the bank manager's guy as Nigel had just been a butcher for years and Mr Goodman the bank manager was, after all, a person of authority.

They went to see Mr Clot. He was a bit shabby, sitting at his desk in what seemed quite a busy office. There were lots of boxes and papers. He was very nice though, asked all sorts of things about the business and even their family, home and mortgage. He said fees would be in the region of £1,000 for the year – a bit more than they were expecting.

They were looking forward to meeting the partner from the other firm tomorrow to compare.

So Mr and Mrs Fryer go and see Mr Hartlet-Brown of Mason, Stone. They are greeted with a nice reception – those fresh flowers are lovely. And then the well-groomed and charming Mr Hartlet-Brown ushers them into a board room, with fresh coffee and biscuits brought in by a very efficient-looking assistant. This is so much better than that other place, this must mean they are better accountants – the Fryers think. Mr Hartlet-Brown says his firm has been established for many years and has experts in all departments so can deal with any issues. He does not ask too much, not like Mr Clot who seemed a bit too searching in his questions. Mr Hartlet-Brown says his charges are based on the time it takes. 'Well what could be fairer that?' the Fryers think 'We want this guy. He doesn't need to know much about us because he knows what to do.'

That's it! Logic has gone, beliefs will be reinforced, prejudices bolstered – *myside bias* has kicked in. They think 'Of course the bank manager knew the best.'

Mr Harlet-Brown says 'We should be starting straight away' so they accept his advice and confirm on the spot that they would like Mason, Stone to act for them. Mr and Mrs Fryer have been sold and effectively stitched-up without even an estimate of price. Mr Hartlet-Brown phones up Mr Goodman and thanks him for the recommendation. He then calls up his wine company and orders a case of champagne to be delivered to Mr Goodman. Mr Goodman and his wife enjoy the wine and make a mental note to send more clients to Hartlet-Brown.

Has that recommendation worked for Mr and Mrs Fryer? They believe they are signing up the firm that is the tops. They instinctively know that they will be paying more but they feel they are getting the best – a proper job, so it's worth it. But are they? Mr Clot's advice might have developed into the **favoured** type in the example coming up in the next couple of pages, leading to £1,000's of savings.

So would not Mr Clot (who wanted to know all about them and gave a fixed price) been a better choice? And so maybe given more 'edgy' tax-saving advice at a better price. They will never know.

They will more than likely stay with Mason, Stone for many years knowing no difference. The firm will give them the **standard professional coverage** year after year and that will be fine. If no mistakes rear their head the Fryers will be satisfied, feeling they are getting the best. However, if a mistake comes to light they might get disillusioned.

I once took over a client from a London City firm which had told the client that the sale of goodwill was taxable even though they had not received the money. The client queried it and the accountant took specialist advice which confirmed what they had said – then charged the client extra. When the accountant did the accounts he forgot to implement his own costly advice and the client paid the wrong tax. The client was suddenly disillusioned with all his work.

CONFLICTING ADVICE

Some might feel justifiably that the advice should be the same whichever accountant they choose. Why should our Mr Clot's advice be any different from Mr Hartlet-Brown's? It's either right or wrong surely?

If only it was that simple.

Some tax stuff is simple and right or wrong. But you do not have to stray too far away from the straightforward to enter a grey area where tax advice may differ from one advisor to another.

When you come across a commercial situation infused with tax issues and serious financial implications, a slight difference in direction on the advice front can make a major difference to the end of year outcome, actually moving from in your favour to against it. In tricky situations, the accountant's natural cautiousness can rear its head and that will come first, since no comeback is ever wanted – **standard professional coverage** comes to his rescue. The alternative – more risky – move that could have saved you thousands will be dismissed.

It is at these decisive points when the advice given can have vital implications; and when your original choice of firm, hand in hand with your partner relationship, will pay dividends (literally perhaps) or not.

If you are following tips in this book to establish yourself as that **favoured client** as opposed to getting the indifferent **standard professional coverage** you might just come across situations where a huge difference could be made. To illustrate this let's consider the following real-life example.

Small business

We have a small business – a children's book publisher, with about ten staff working for it. There will be writers, illustrators, designers and editors. Historically they have been self-employed and the owner has paid them for the days they work, not the same amounts each month but certainly on a regular basis. One senior editor is self-employed but has a company car. The owner knows other businesses similar to his where everybody is on the payroll. The owner raises the situation with his accountant. 'I am worried about HMRC finding out. What should I be doing?' he asks.

The standard professional coverage advice

In a larger or medium firm such a query would tend to be dealt with by a manager, not a partner – and possibly someone who the owner has not had a lot of contact with. Some firms might say, 'You need to speak to our PAYE specialist.' The largish firm's employee will be very careful about giving advice that might be called into question and will err on the side of caution. He will tend to give the safe, textbook answer.

That answer is not good news for the owner. His advice could be that the owner will be in breach of the PAYE rules and he must put all the staff on the payroll immediately. The extra cost of this would be about 12% on National Insurance and an extra 10% that he would have to pay the employees to cover the effect of lowering their take-home pay.

This is a dismal situation, as the owner will be faced with an increase of 22% in his wages bill.

The favoured client advice

If your firm is one with whom you have built a relationship, maybe a small practice or a particular partner you know well, you should address this query to that person, the partner who knows you. He will have more insight into your position, being a small-business owner himself rather than an employee, and he should tend to be sympathetic. He will immediately understand the situation you are faced with. If he is experienced he will be on the lookout for solutions for you from the minute you start to explain the problem.

Because the 22% hike might actually cripple the business altogether, the partner should look for a way you can carry on but stay inside the regulations. While the other firm's recommendations will be cut and dried, your favoured partner should be more flexible.

He might suggest making a few changes so that, if you were challenged, you had an argument to put forward to refute the taxman's claim. It may not be 100% certain but if you get these changes in place your business may carry on rather than nosedive into losses. This is the advice a small business needs.

So the partner might say, 'First, you can't give self-employed staff a car. That is out of the question, so sell it to them. Second, you need to follow the rules on the HMRC website for self-employed vs employed people. In the IR35 section (put that in the search engine) you will find a points-scoring system for self-employment. Get those "staff" on contracts that can qualify on the points. If they cannot qualify then they will have to go on PAYE, but make a few changes to try and get them all to qualify.'

In other words, *adapt and change* to fit the taxman's self-employed profile. This way the arrangement could continue for many years. So your small firm's advice may have saved you 22% on your annual £100,000 wage bill. That is £22,000 per year.

Your other firm meting out the **standard professional coverage** would have cost you £22k extra per year, and no doubt higher fees as well.

BEWARE OF THE EXPERTS

Some firms will claim to be specialists in particular areas. There is a saying in accountancy – two clients in the same business and you are a specialist, three and you are an expert.

When I started up, my first client was an old flatmate, a photographer. A few months later his friend – another photographer – came over to me; by then, I was a specialist in their eyes. Not long after I got another colleague of theirs. There was no particular expertise needed for photographers' accounts but they thought I had some expert knowledge that they needed.

There are only a few professions where specialist accountants are useful. These can include doctors, entertainers and charities, to cite some. Certain firms do home in on specialist markets. I have come across accountancy firms the majority of whose clientele are one trade, say dentists or taxi drivers. They will have a tried and tested formula for dealing with that particular trade. This can work to your advantage. The main thing to watch out for is price. If it seems reasonable then you could be better off with a specialist.

In the entertainment world, specialist entertainment accountants can carry out services for the type of clients of which other accountants have little experience. Many entertainers want nothing to do with the money side, do not want to write cheques or open any letters that contain a bill. A provincial, high-street-type accountant might find this strange, whereas the specialist accountant greets this with open arms. He'll have his system of dealing with it and can charge handsomely for it. Provided he keeps his client away from all money and manages his client's expectations, he is onto a winner.

There are cases where this has backfired but, generally, using a regulated accountancy firm to control their money is a safe bet for such clients and far better than handing all over to an unqualified, unregulated music business manager.

THE FIRM

If you want to get the right firm and the right accountant then do not leave it till the last minute to appoint one. That will limit your choice and pressurise you into accepting basically the first 'through the door'. This is an important appointment, so go and see them before your tax or company affairs are so urgent that you need the work doing yesterday.

So you are now armed to make the decision on who to choose. You are giving it the time it deserves. You have sized up the various firms, sought some recommendations, looked at their websites. Now you need to go and see three. If possible get three recommendations. Keep an open mind till you have seen them all. Ask similar questions and observe.

Your work of building your good accountant has just started.

5

JUDGEMENT

Having picked out your type of firm, you now have the challenging task of making contact with your chosen accountant to set the ball rolling. This will generally be by phone. You ring up for an appointment, either following a recommendation to a particular person or expecting to be directed to the person who in that firm is best suited to your affairs. Most accountants will give a first meeting free of charge – if they don't it's a warning sign. Some will even come to your premises without charging if your fee looks worth it.

Right from the moment when the phone is answered you will subconsciously be making critical assessments. After all, until you sign on the dotted line you could easily go to another. So the tentacles are out from the second that first phone call is made, and how the phone is answered can shape your view. Accountants know this and it should always be answered well. It may be brash or functional; that's okay.

It does not matter if the partner is there when you phone or not. That is random and irrelevant. In one way if you get straight through to them you are actually less well informed. This is because it is helpful to judge how quickly they might get back to you.

Let's say they are not there and you have to leave a message. 'I am calling up to see if you could become my new accountant,' you might say. The response might be: 'Oh you need to speak to David Smith. He is not here at the moment but I will message him and he should call you back.'

Here you have a judgement. How long before he calls you back? Should it be one hour, one day, or two days? How long should you give before the length of time is unreasonable?

There is a dilemma here: how busy do you want your accountant to be? If your accountant is always available, it follows he is not that busy. It follows from that that he can't be that good.

There is also a saying: 'I had a good accountant but I could never get hold of him so I got another.' Then that is too busy. You need the happy medium: he is busy but he always gets back to you. So I would say the appropriate response time is later that day or, if you called in the afternoon, the following morning. It may well be earlier, accountants can be in and out of meetings but a general practitioner is unlikely to be tied up all day without being able to take a break and check his calls and messages.

APPEARANCES

I had a client couple for many years who were fantastic clients and became good friends. They ran a number of businesses. The husband later died and in conversation the widow told me that when I first pulled up outside their offices she had looked out of the window and remarked to her husband, 'He must be good – he drives a black **BMW**.' (It was actually a black *Fiat* that looked like a *BMW*.) They were wrong in their reasoning but right 'of course' in their choice. Appearances do (wrongly) matter.

The reception area will indicate to you the general 'attitude' of the firm as set by the partners/directors. Is it flash or functional? Is it clean or dusty? Does it smack of overheads or economy? You can get an idea of how your service will be and how you will be charged by the type of reception you are sitting in.

For years my firm never really bothered with a reception area and we did not have a dedicated receptionist because all our staff were continuously working. Clients were generally never kept waiting, they were shown directly into our meeting room and one of the partners would greet the new client straight away. This showed three things:

1. We kept overheads low, which ultimately gets reflected in charges
2. We did not keep clients waiting, we valued their time
3. We relied on our service to speak for itself

Big Four accountants have lavish receptions and 'like their receptionists in high heels'. London West End firms have slick receptions showing MTV or News 24. While you are sitting there, size it all up. Does the receptionist have work other than sitting there dolled-up waiting for the phone to ring? If not, you are the one who will be paying for it.

FIRST CONSULTATION

It is at this first meeting you are likely to heavily shape your decision as to the person or firm to whom you are going to entrust your financial affairs. The first impressions cliché applies.

However, the client is in a difficult situation with regard to making an informed choice because the accountant will be putting on a front, be on his guard. Be careful not to be impressed by random things. These are actually really insignificant but because of a lack of real value information they take on the role of evidence of 'quality' by default. Keep an open mind, at the start anyway.

But, how an earth then are you going to make the right choice? There is no trial period, no yardstick, no independent assessment and no one to guide you. You are pretty well on your own, with little to go on. A business decision where you're taking pot luck is not the best of ways. Especially in financial areas. The accountant will be selling, selling and selling himself and his firm. Make no mistake, he is only in the meeting with you to sign you up. This could be your first meeting with 'an accountant' but remember he has done loads of these 'new client' meetings. He has heard it all before.

Many clients have come to me and I instinctively know they are going to 'sign up'. I only have to be pleasant, sound interesting, be passionate and the client is mine. But occasionally a new client will come and start asking some searching questions. Suddenly I become very awake and take my response to another level. After taking on that client I make a mental note to ensure everything is done to a high standard for him, and that includes advice. You want to be in that bag.

So you must not 'nod' yourself in. Don't make it too easy. Be questioning and discerning. Trying the same questions on two accountants might yield answers that are interesting or confusing.

One new client came to me and said 'I like to change my accountant every three years.' That was an interesting comment I had never heard before. What he was getting at was the complacency that can set in (which we address later). The comment stuck with me but actually he did stay longer than three years; in fact, until he retired.

YOUR OWN MAN

Whatever the size of the firm, or its reputation, you need to get to that accountant who will principally be in charge of your affairs; someone who will get to know you and your circumstances. A person in this role is more likely to give you the best service rather than service to a formula, remote accounting or by rotating staff. So it is him or her that really matters rather than their surroundings. It is he who will direct the service you get, while others in the firm follow his lead. So when you get to meet this guy, look for the following:

Experience

You need to know he has done it before. Experience counts. It will give you that extra security. Age is a pretty good guide but don't be afraid to ask 'How long have you been here? I bet you have been doing this for years.' Experience will also give him that extra edge when it comes to sailing close to the wind. Inexperienced accountants can be over-cautious – to your financial detriment. Young guys can be slick and clever but you generally need a steady hand. Experience is often underestimated..

Skill

You need to feel he has the skills necessary for what is a technical and serious job. He should have a proper professional qualification, rather than a *Mickey Mouse* one. Ask him what his qualifications are. What do the letters actually stand for? You should understand this at least. You don't engage a medical consultant without fully believing he has the right qualifications. So which regulated body supervises the work of this accountant? Is he in one of the main bodies, with the letters ACA/FCA (*Institute of Chartered Accountants*) or an ACCA/FCCA (*Chartered Certified Accountants*)? That's the first check. If one of those then all should be well on that front. Be wary of 'management accountants' as they are a different breed. Maybe they left company accounting for some dubious reason. Be wary too of anyone with an apparent string of other letters.

Integrity

An essential quality in your accountant. Most have it, a few don't, and a greater few will bend it to make an increased profit. A suit may look the part but the better ones may not generally wear a tie. He may be so good he comes in smart jeans and a jacket. But listen and evaluate what they say on an 'integrity' basis. If he says, 'Keep cash out of the books so I don't see it...' BEWARE. Look for honesty. Look for it in things you can judge. Does he dress honestly? Do you feel he is talking down to you?

Passion

This is a great seller as it's infectious. If you see passion in your accountant's eyes for what he does, you feel good. An accountant that refers to his work as 'boring' or 'compliance work' is not going to inspire you. Compliance work is the routine stuff that has to be done. Essentially that boils down to form-filling. If he says 'I'm only here on Tuesday, Wednesday and Thursday', it may be a warning sign – if he is passionate he will be available for you when you need him, within reason.

Resources

Larger firms make great play of all their departments but these services are also available to the small accountant who brings in specialists, often at a more competitive cost. Beware of claims to be part of a network as this is unlikely to be relevant to most clients. Beware of claims that their firm is better than others – no real professional should say that.

Continuity

You need to feel secure that he is going to be around next year and the years after. With chartered accountants you get the security of their regulating body, which inspects and monitors members so your files should be protected. Remember, chartered accountants have to have procedures in place to protect your files if they fall ill or run off with their secretary.

Valued

Are you going to be looked after by this person or thrown to the lions, i.e. the trainees? You don't want just a figurehead, you want the considered overview, even if only once a year, by the person you have chosen to be your accountant. Make sure you have chosen the right size of firm to find your man. Some large firms can put their most personable man as a figurehead, a smoothie who won't actually work on your affairs as these will be farmed out. You don't really want that as it defeats our objectives. The glib assurance *you will get a dedicated accountant looking after you* are pretty worthless words.

DO THEY GET TO KNOW YOU?

A good accountant needs to be fully aware of your background to advise you properly. This is where the face-to-face accountant really can score as opposed to the *remote* (web-based) accountant. Your accountant should *get to know you*.

After many years, the *Financial Services Authority* (FCA now) did finally introduce strict rules forcing financial advisors to get to know their clients. This was known as KYC, which stands for *Know Your Client*, where you do a full appraisal of their circumstances before giving any advice. Total sense. There are no such mandatory rules for accountants but if they are to give best advice they must know their client's circumstances. If you are not asked, it's a warning sign. Really good accountants may visit their client's business premises some time during the first year. The accountant can gain a better idea of who you are and what advice you will need from a visit to you on your home ground.

Visiting clients at their home or business premises not only builds better rapport but also helps the accountant see more of what goes on. He takes things in subconsciously that enable him to give tailored and effective advice.

Once, I went to see a client at his home, from where he ran his business. He showed me around and we came to the new garage he had had built, which he used for storage of business goods for resale. It was at his home so he had not considered it part of his business even though he fully used it to store his goods in.

I asked who paid for the garage. He said, 'We got an extra mortgage.' Immediately I said, 'Well, we will put through the interest on the loan as a business expense, claim the VAT back on the build and claim some capital allowances each year.' He saved over £5,000 in tax just because I went to his home.

The accountant you go and see needs to be asking about *you* and not quite so much talking about *them* and how good they are. Like our Mr Clot, the apparently uninspiring accountant who wanted to know all about his potential client so he could give best advice. The Fryer's in their ignorance took it as intrusive.

FREE ADVICE

Once the accountant has asked you some questions about yourself and your business in his patter does he offer some advice, or is it just about how good he is?

If he is competent there should be some suggestion he could make. Not only in tax saving, but bookkeeping, computing, considerations on limited companies, partnerships, filing deadlines, penalties, tax rates, VAT or just timing of doing your accounts. Look for some *advice* forthcoming on something. Question – is he generous with his advice or not? Size him up.

He should be. After all, he is there giving up his time anyway so it costs nothing extra to give you a few bits of helpful advice, even if you don't come to him.

You don't want grandiose claims like 'I can get you to pay *no* tax' – that may indicate a scam. No, look for small bits of help.

If he seems mean with this at this stage and you feel that he is not giving you anything to take away, it could indicate that he will be mean when you are a client – to the extent that you get absolutely nothing unless you pay for it. Some accountants have that attitude inbuilt, there is no give unless there is there is plenty of take. You do not want to get into a situation where take assumes the controlling role. You want a fair deal, not one that is weighted against you. So if you get a few 'tips' at that first meeting it's a good sign.

If you don't, it's either because he is not switched on enough to think of any or it's a sign of meanness. So look for the 'tips'. Size this one up carefully.

SKILLED OPERATORS

Remember, as we said, the accountant you see will most likely have done this before and be skilled at dealing with new clients. He will have heard all the general questions before and have stock answers. But a really smart operator will latch on to your concerns, sense an issue or problem, then show you how his firm is particularly good at solving it for you – in the best way and in your best interests. This is the classic sales technic:

1. Identify a problem

2. Emphasise the threats

3. Offer the solution

Works every time.

When people say to me 'I've got a great accountant', I smile to myself and think '*Yes*, great at PR!'

So ask yourself if he is really interested in talking to you. Does he dismiss your questions? Is he eager to get back on track, deal only with accountancy points and bring the meeting to an end as soon as possible?

Skilled accountants will actually do both. They will impart an interest in you personally for a limited time, bringing the discussion back to the points in hand having built up a rapport with you.

Accountants like these are firmly in command of the situation. Be wary of being led by skilled operators, though, and make sure your questions and queries are adequately answered.

You won't know the technical bits, so an accountant experienced in PR will know exactly the right answers to give you to indicate that this is the right firm for you. He will sing the praise of his firm, his clients, his staff, his experience, his training and back-up, his proactivity, his timing and more.

But do be wary of answers that always seem to lead back to a solution offered only by his firm.

COMBAT THE SKILL

When you are up against someone very skilled then try a few 'off beat' type questions and see his reaction.

- How many partners are there in the firm?
- How long have you been in these offices?
- Will you be dealing personally with my accounts?
- Could I be introduced to the manager that I will be dealing with?
- How many clients of my size do you have?
- Is your firm the right size for my business?
- Do you charge for phone calls?
- Can my fee be fixed?

JUDGE BY QUESTIONS

Hence with all this going on, and for the guy that seems to have all the answers to your questions, you must seriously look at what he is asking you. So let's analyse it.

Does he convey a genuine level of interest? Does he home in on a bit of detail to see how you are different? Do you have the feeling he understands you? If at the end of the meeting you feel he does not, be careful. You will probably not have another meeting for a while so this may be your last chance.

Look at his questions more than his answers. Has he asked enough to really understand your affairs? Has he asked about your family situation, because knowledge of this can give tax advantages? Has he asked about your future business plans?

His questions are vital. They direct the meeting, which he should be doing. So ask yourself, has he asked enough questions?

NOTES OF MEETING

Does he make notes at the meeting? The answer should be yes. The correct way would be to start by just talking generally and then gradually start making some notes. He could say 'I just want to take down a few details now.' If he starts writing furiously at the start he is probably lacking in experience. Notes should be made, but in moderation.

When you make an individual point about the business he should note it down. For example, 'We use about six permanent subcontractors at the moment' should be on his notes of the meeting.

They are his file notes, you should not expect a copy.

ARE THEY MARKETING TOO MUCH?

As we have said, recommendations have traditionally been the strongest source of quality clients from the accountant's point of view. They will always be the preferred choice for new business. Traditional or online marketing, will tend to indicate they are not getting enough ongoing referrals; hence they will market themselves if their organic growth is inadequate.

Recent years have seen a tailing-off of recommendations and an increase in marketing. Some accountants have embraced social networking marketing, such as *Google, LinkedIn, Bing, Facebook, Experian, Scoot* and *Twitter*. Some pay to be on networks such as *VouchedFor*. You may well come across an accountant this way. But this marketing requires extra effort, which for an accountant is time – time when he could otherwise be using his expertise doing clients' work and earning fees.

So try and access how much marketing your accountant does. If it's a lot, perhaps his product is no good and that's why he's doing so much. Every accountant knows that clients that come in response to advertising are not of the same quality as clients that are recommended. They tend to be shop-arounders, are more demanding and questioning on fees. Firms by nature prefer unquestioning clients, which is why this multi-marketing form of attracting clients tends to be a last resort.

The aggressive marketer may be up high on *Google*, advertise locally, hold seminars and may even have cold-called you, but what are the reasons for this? Are they so short of recommendations? Do they want to expand quickly? If the answers to these questions are yes, then you need to consider how this may impact on your service and quality of advice.

Accountants do, however, need some new clients unless they are about to retire. This is because clients die, go bust or get taken over, or at worst change to another accountant (not always for the right reasons). So you could expect some marketing directed towards new business, such as an up-to-date website, or attending a local business network or giving talks. Moderate PR is fine, just not too much.

LOW-BALLING

This is a term given to under-quoting to get a new client, with the underlying intention of gradually putting up their fees. You go to see a potential new accountant and he asks what your current accountant is charging. You say £x and he says, 'We can do it for half that'. You think 'This is a no-brainer'. But gradually over the years, your fees creep up.

If you speak to another accountant, they will almost certainly say your current fees are too high, and if they want your business they may well do this *low ball*. Remember, accountancy services are not like a quote from a builder for a set job. It's a quote for the start of a long-term relationship. The insurance industry has been uncovered for charging new customers much less than existing customers, putting their premiums up year by year as a reverse loyalty reward to themselves. This was easy to spot by regulators and media watchdogs – but it's much harder to detect with accountants.

Your accountant may find a valid-sounding reason for putting your fees up the minute you are hooked. If he says that it's taken a long time this year because the books were a mess and did not balance properly, how are you to know whether that is genuine or an exaggeration in justification of fees? Most properly-qualified accountants are trained in a code of ethics and are generally professional and honest with HMRC and clients. But some are not and could low ball to the extreme.

So be careful of fees that seems too good to be true. *If it's too good to be true, then it probably is* – as the saying goes.

INTUITION

'Trust your hunches. They are usually based on facts filed away just below the conscious level.' – someone said somewhere.

Of course, intuition is an inexact science and therefore comes only *after* all my tips for sizing things up, which I hope you have taken on board.

When you have done all the rational things, go with your hunch – your educated guess as to who is going to be right for you. The person and firm you have chosen obviously have the basic things you need, so now they are ready to be moulded into your 'good' accountant.

One humorous tip I read once was to pick an accountant with the same name as you – as at least then you won't be forgotten. There is a message there somewhere.

6

TIED-UP

Most professionals – solicitors, architects, chartered surveyors, estate agents and so on – have a standard way of covering themselves contractually with their clients. We have got used to this, and it is not only professionals but many business services also have 'terms and conditions'. We are so used to it that it is expected, to the extent that it is now so standard that it has become irrelevant and not worthy of scrutiny.

Professionals fall into a pattern and get clients to sign their terms and conditions in a friendly letter form. The practice is so prevalent that not enough heed is given to what is signed. Most businesses, companies or self-employed people will have dealt with other professionals so it's not a surprise to get a letter, often you are just waiting for it to come. It is virtually without exception just standard practice to get a signature accepting the terms without a quibble.

Indeed why should they quibble? This is the start of a great relationship and optimism prevails and *he is such a nice man*. Things going wrong is not on the menu.

Solicitors cheekily call it their 'client care letter' – what clever legal eagle thought that phrase up? Accountants, are more straightforward perhaps and describe this as the 'letter of engagement'. A totally honest name, though, would be 'your contract and our terms'.

LOOK AT THE ENDING FIRST

Believe it or not, it is recommended chartered accountancy practice to also offer a 'letter of disengagement' for clients to sign when they leave.

What on earth is this? There is no fixed term of engagement (usually) so it can be terminated by any party at any time, without notice. So what is the accountant getting at here?

No client in their right mind would sign it and I believe virtually none do. The optimism and urgency has gone and so has that 'nice man' syndrome. So the slightest inclination to do the accountant's bidding and sign such a ridiculously restrictive document has evaporated for ever. Most partings from accountants are under a cloud anyway.

The ICAEW-recommended contents of this disengagement letter are (paraphrased in my words) to:

(a) Remind you that you signed the restrictive terms and conditions at the outset (ha ha!).
(b) Say your records will be incinerated if you don't come grovelling to our offices and get them.
(c) Say any advice we gave was only for you, so don't go shouting your mouth off to others.
(d) Ask you to 'hold us harmless' as we are such gentle folk.
(e) Say there could be extra fees due. What a surprise!

The ICAEW guidance goes on to say (accountants are ever practical):

'Look, no one is likely to sign this but send it out anyway as it could have some legal standing if it comes to a fight.' So that's the ending you can expect, but let's start at the beginning.

THE LETTER OF ENGAGEMENT

So under the guise of their professional bodies' *ethics* and *'best practice'* out comes this document at the start of the relationship in the form of a friendly letter.

After the polite and friendly start you are already bored. You know what they are going to say and that they will get a bit technical with stuff you really just want them to deal with. So the stuff in the middle you are unlikely to read – and they are not that keen for you to do so; they will be happy if you just flick to the end and sign it and send it back.

You are in a hurry for them to get on with the urgent matters for which you have hired them. Not many go and engage an accountant in advance (even though this is the most sensible route, as I advised earlier in this book).

Each January, just before the self-assessment deadline, accountants get their biggest influx of new clients and everyone is in a hurry to get their tax done. So you sign up and send back – without perhaps fully appreciating that the letter is in fact a formal legal contract.

As you have more or less already engaged the accountant, signing this just seems like a small formality before you get on with the real business of your accounts and tax.

The contract you are signing will ensure the firm's own position is well protected in the event of a falling-out between you. It is designed by them for them.

It might say something like this:

BEAN, COUNTER & PARTNERS LLP

Chartered Accountants

Top Floor
9a High Street
Tickenham

Dear John,

LETTER OF ENGAGEMENT

We are pleased to be able to offer you our services for your company and personal tax which we set out below. We would be grateful if you could sign one copy of this letter and return it to us for our files ...

[Don't worry about this technical middle bit or the extinguishing of your rights]

... Please do not hesitate to contact me if you have any queries or questions. Please sign and date the extra copy and return it to us. We look forward to assisting you in every way with your and your company's affairs.

Simon Bean ACA
BEAN, COUNTER & PARTNERS LLP

**I have read and understood this letter
and agree with its contents**

.... John So-Willing

LOADED DICE?

Unfortunately, things are stacked against you at this point. We have said about your eagerness to sign, ignoring the detailed conditions, and to get on with the 'important things'. The other issue is the fact that you cannot practically complain at this 'standard' contract of terms, even if you disagree with them. It is effectively a 'non-negotiable' contract. Remember *British Telecom* – once you had made the first call you were locked in to their terms you had never read.

If you do complain about them at this early stage then red flags are likely to go up as 99% of clients do not. At worst the accountant will turn round and say that he will not act for you unless you sign. You then either have to find another (and get the same type of letter) or stumble on in the muddied water. However, if you are a client that the accountant really wants – and that is only one thing, a client that will pay fees that produce super profits – then you may be able to get it adjusted. Realistically speaking, this type of client is one in a million.

SCOPE OF LETTER

The letter should cover four basic points:
1. It should identify the client. Either in a personal capacity, a partnership or a limited company. If the accountant acts for a group of companies one 'group' letter may suffice.
2. It should define the scope of the work to be carried out and the terms under which it is done.
3. It should cover the firm's responsibilities and what is expected of the client.
4. It should set out *fees*.

FEES

Most disputes are around the fees issue and the letter will address this in various forms of detail. The *Institute of Chartered Accountants'* sample engagement letter that they had on their website has about 10 points under the heading 'Fees and Payment Terms'.

It may be a surprise to some clients just what the Institute recommends its members say to clients on fees. I have set out below my interpretation of the recommended terms:

- Fees are based on time, skill, responsibility, importance, value and risk **so basically anything we can dream up**
- We can charge **what we like**
- If we give you an estimate **it doesn't count**
- If we give you a fixed fee **we can alter it**
- If you have HMRC investigation insurance **you are still liable for our fees**
- We can **add** disbursements and third party charges
- We can ask for money **in advance and by direct debit**
- We can **charge interest**

Then a bombshell at the end:

- If you do not complain within 21 days **you are prohibited** from complaining

And then the final shock – a clause which purports to undermine the basis of limited liability:

- If your company does not pay, **you must pay personally**

SAMPLE TERMS

Firms have some discretion on which of these recommendations to include. My firm sends out terms that we think are fair but protect our interests from clients who feel they could use our time without paying for it. What follows below is my firm's letter of engagement and terms. Never, though, in all the years with our many and varied clients, have we had to revert to the terms to settle an issue.

Our engagement

Our work involves what is necessary to competently look after and keep you advised on your affairs. Work varies with your instructions which it is agreed may be given by tel/email/writing to our offices (not to mobiles or by text message). Consultancy services supplied by way of retainer are for advice given generally at meetings and we do not take over any responsibilities for implementation. On commencing or continuing to use our services these terms are deemed to apply and we carry out our work for you on the basis you accept our charges as set out here. Files can be inspected by our Institute and are normally destroyed after six years. On disengagement a final bill will be rendered on a time basis up to the date of disengagement. This must be paid before any information is collated and passed on. Following payment all your information will be supplied within 15 working days. You must arrange collection of your accounting records. Any records left and not collected will be destroyed after six months.

Standard basis of charges

*Our fees are charged within the guidelines of our Institute and are computed on the basis of the time spent on your affairs. The **total** time spent by partners and staff is charged at an hourly rate based on the seniority of the person undertaking* *the work. These charge-out rates start at £40/hr for junior staff to £196/hr for a senior partner. The total **time** expended, recorded in ¼ hour units, will represent the chargeable **time** on your affairs before additional costs or charges. This **time** can include meetings, calls or emails, also travelling or delays, monitoring your affairs, reviewing papers or compliance and money laundering requirements.*

Payment terms

It is agreed to pay our invoices/demands within 14 days or raise any query in writing within that time. If our invoice is not paid following a reminder it is agreed we may cease work, exercise a general lien and/or not supply information until settled. 'On account' invoices are to be paid immediately in order for the work to be continued without delay. Our bills that are sent out with accounts are fully due when raised irrespective of the filing and tax work that continues afterwards.

Fixed price quotes (if applies)

If a fixed price is given this will be in writing and state the work it covers. Fixed prices are based on the information given to us and assume you keep good honest records of all transactions. Fixed prices cover the work specified only. If you instigate any other use of our time it will be charged for in accord with the standard basis above, If you have been quoted a fixed fee and you dis-engage us before we can complete the work or we are frustrated in any way from continuing then our charges will fall to be based on the total time involved on your affairs from the outset, including all meeting, travel, emails, calls and work carried out. Should extra work be necessary on your affairs by factors outside our control or not allowed for in the quote or fixed price then this will be billed in accordance with our standard basis for the time spent as detailed above.

Personal Tax Return Questionnaire and Engagement Terms update (if applies)

Each April we send out a questionnaire which we ask you to complete. This enables us to deal with your affairs more efficiently and keep our costs to you down. We will take the information you give us as full disclosure unless we are aware of any contradictory facts.

Confidentiality

While some clients' names are generally known all your affairs are confidential. If we receive references/requests for you which appear to be in good faith and for your benefit you authorise us to divulge your details at our discretion without any further confirmation. We may discuss/disclose matters with your spouse/partner/co-directors or others expected to have your confidence unless notified otherwise in writing.

Representations given to us and your books and accounting records

We will prepare accounts and tax returns on the basis of your records and/or other information given to us. Some items may be open to interpretation or lack back-up. We will take the prima face view that these are valid expenses on your behalf. HMRC may not agree and you accept this as a risk. You understand that YOU are responsible for keeping proper records and you can ask us for guidance on the rules at any time.

Tax Investigations, deadlines and penalties

If you are the subject of an HMRC investigation this will entail extra costs which can start at £100/m for small clients. We may request 'on account' fees. To avoid late penalties you *must ensure that all necessary documents are with us eight weeks before any deadlines of which <u>you</u> must make yourself aware – just ask us. Penalties apply for incomplete record-keeping now so please keep good records of all income and expenditure.*

Financial Services and Data Protection Act 1998

We are able to introduce you to IFA's covering pensions, permanent health insurance, life cover etc. While we do not recommend specific products we can advise on how these are relevant to your needs and their affordability for you. We retain information under the Data Processing Act 1998. You have right of access, our Data Controller is xxxx. Files are kept for six years.

Commissions received, Interest payable and tax refunds

We can accept any tax refunds and deduct our fees (from you or any company in which you have an interest). If we receive any commissions it is agreed that we will retain these. Any interest earned on client monies held will not be paid unless you request that a separate account is opened.

VAT for self-employed and companies

If you are un-registered you <u>must monitor your own turnover</u> for registration purposes on a month to month basis. It is your responsibility for <u>all</u> VAT registration and compliance matters. After registration if you subscribe to our quarterly VAT service then we will oversee your VAT liabilities.

Tax credits, class 2 National Insurance (if self-employed) and miscellaneous income

We do not take on any responsibility for any Employment legislation, Tax Credits, Benefits, Grants, Class 2 National

Insurance weekly fixed amount. You need to deal with these matters yourself.

Important changes in your circumstances

It is your total responsibility to advise us <u>in writing</u> of any changes of <u>address, telephones, mobiles, emails</u>.

PAYE, registration, P11(D) forms, CIS monthly returns and company secretarial/ dividend documentation

If any of these apply to you we <u>do not </u>deal with these automatically so you must monitor your own compliance in these areas. If you wish us to deal with any of them then they will be undertaken on receipt of your specific instructions and our separate confirmation in writing.

Giving good service and resolving complaints without proceedings

You agree to firstly address any complaint to xxxxxxx. If you become aware of any errors it is agreed that you will first raise these with us and give time for their correction and opportunity to discuss them and compromise or settle. It is agreed that any complaint not settled will be referred to the Institute of CA's who have a fee arbitration, compensation and a complaint resolution system, before further action is initiated. Our insurer giving worldwide cover excluding US is xxxxxxxxxxx London EC3.

Third party liability

We prepare accounts for HMRC, Companies House requirements and the shareholders and directors. We accept no responsibility to other parties unless you agree this with us in writing. We do not carry out/advise on valuations.

Applicable law, money laundering regulations and disclosure policy

These engagement terms shall continue unless superseded until we are dis-instructed and shall be governed by, and construed in accordance with English Law decided in their courts. Your business may need money laundering registration which is <u>your responsibility</u>.

Most of this letter is designed to protect us from claims, not to tie up the client. I don't think 95% of clients ever read it.

THE SYSTEM

So that's the upshot of your engagement, and in the current system you are stuck with it. As I said, complain and be damned. So what do you do?

The only recommendation I can give is:

> In the fees section add (in your own small writing) a really brief comment
>
> *as per quote*
>
> and separately (by email, say) get the fees and work confirmed.

7

FEES

Accountancy is a classic service-based industry. There is no manufacturing, no physical product to sell, no goods to move, no stock to hold. What is sold is *time*. Everything reverts back to time. Time is king. There are only so many hours in the working day for the partner and his staff.

These hours are all there is to generate the fees to pay for everything. So it is important that these hours are maximised and effectively charged out to clients.

The charging of hours is most straightforward for the accounts production and audit staff. They can work all day on one client and so their 7 hours all get charged to that client. Simple.

For the partner it becomes much more complicated. He may get 20 phone calls in a day, half from clients half from non-clients, and masses of emails. He has his administration to do in the firm, personnel and business matters to deal with, all eating into his daily time. At the day's end he may feel he has only done three hours chargeable time.

So those three hours have to earn and the clients that have taken up that three hours have to pay.

So the first thing to remember is **Do not waste your partner's time** – you will pay for doing so.

Just remember your accountant will be time-conscious to the extreme. He wants to recoup his time hand-in-hand with you feeling to a certain extent 'satisfied'.

You might phone up, for example, unexpectedly interrupting your accountant. He is likely to be in the middle of a complicated piece of work (as the things that come to him usually are). But, he will be so polite even though his only real aim will be to get you off the phone as soon as possible and back to finish the job he had started before you phoned with your query.

So make sure your calls are important or urgent. Email if not.

CHARGE-OUT RATES

Time-based fees in an accountancy practice operate through a hierarchal organisation system. Seniority is clearly defined by your charge-out rate, from the lowliest clerk or admin assistant to the highest-paid partner (normally the senior partner). Each of the members of the firm will be allocated a fixed charge-out rate. This will be based on their salary and level of competence integrated with the firm's policy.

A distinction will be made between fee-earners and non-fee-earners in the firm. Examples of non-fee-earners are a general filing clerk, a secretary or PA, who usually play no part in the make-up of your bill. They are usually taken in as a general overhead of the firm.

Your bill will be calculated by reference to the time involved by each member of productive fee-earning staff. Most readers will be familiar with this for their car service which is basically the same method.

A typical structure of charge-out rates per hour based on averages between different sizes of firms might be:

> **Junior clerk** – does basic schedules, photocopying. £15 in a small firm to £100 in a large.
>
> **First grade accounts staff** – does spreadsheets, income and expenditure accounts. £35 in a small firm to £150 in a large.
>
> **Accounts/audit senior/manager** – can do final accounts, supervise staff. £75 in a small firm to £400 in a large.
>
> **Partner** – can vary hugely, from £100 in a very small firm to £1,000 in a large firm.

So how are these charge-out rates calculated? The rule of thumb for the smaller firms has traditionally been to charge fee-earning staff out at three times their hourly salary. The mathematical basis for this system is this covers one for the staff cost, one for the overhead cost and one for the profit. Partners tend to be charged according to their experience, and by comparison with other firms.

Rates we can see vary widely but tend to follow the size of the firm you are dealing with. Partners in the very large firms can be charged out at as much as five times the rates of a very small firm. The large firms will set their rates in line with the other large firms, whereas smaller firms will tend to use their own cost base to set their rates.

THE LEDGER

So you can see from the above why the time has to be recorded to calculate the fee. Most accountants have a computer system that does just that. Each fee-earner will complete a 'time sheet', usually on a weekly basis, for input into a computer program which is essentially an A to Z list of clients with the totals of time spent on each client.

Some accountants may a have real-time system which semi-automatically records your time charge. This can be phone calls, emails, reminders, every time your file is accessed, correspondence received from HMRC, meetings – all building up your time record.

The time spent on your affairs will escalate over the year without you even knowing as some of this work happens without your involvement.

When a job is completed the partner will look at the time ledger to see his and his staff's time over the year and any disbursements. He will then get an idea of the cost to be billed to the client. Smaller firms may have had a much simpler version and just kept a note of the time on the file. But whatever method used the firm's time forms the basis for the fee.

DISCRETION

While the time ledger calculates the time cost this might well not be the end of the story. On top of this cost comes the discretion of the partner. A partner will want to maximise fees so if there is a margin to put up the charge he may well do so.

For example, he knows you have had a good year and he has given you one or two pieces of good advice. These have not taken too much of his time but they have been very valuable to you. He may then add on 10% or 30% to the bill. This is the discretionary part. Remember, in the last chapter's *letter of engagement* it says fees can be based on *importance and value*. Such an indefinable concept is hard to pin down and would be hard to argue against in reality.

Sometimes the time calculation can work in your favour. Just because you are on a time basis does not mean to say you will get billed for all the time that has been spent on your affairs. Sometimes time costs can run so high that the bill comes out at much more than the partner feels he can charge the client. This leads to what are called 'time write-offs'.

The time costing could work out at, say, £4,567 but the partner knows that the maximum fee he can charge is £1,500, so he will have to write off a massive £3,067. Consequently he may have some explaining to do to his other partners as to why he has spent the firm's resources on a client that he could not recover on.

If you are that client, look out – because next year you may get a shock. Often staff referred to some jobs as 'loss leaders' if the time costs continually went unrecovered year after year. Because of these loss leaders, unfortunately there is bound to be a tendency to uplift fees on other clients to compensate wherever your accountant can.

THE 'F' WORD

It should not come as a surprise to learn that fees can be the most important factor to your accountant. Don't make the mistake of thinking he wants to deal with you because you (or your business) are interesting. However exciting your business may be to you, the bottom line is that the firm is only interested in their profit. The partner will be constantly 'on guard' against any signs that you might renege on your fees. You can have a minor falling-out that escalates over time. Your accountant is well aware that a disagreement can lead to resentment and negative feelings and that there are plenty more fish in the sea when it comes to accountants, so he will be defensive from the start.

THE UPPER HAND

Accountants know that fees are a sensitive area for most so will tend to avoid airing the subject if possible. In some cases you may have to take the initiative and broach the subject. The 'just based on time' is not good enough. You need to pin them down and put them on the spot. A good time to do this is before that letter of engagement comes. As we said at the end of the previous chapter, you could add on that letter somewhere 'as per email' / 'as per meeting'.

So if you get a quote in the meeting, you might like to jot it down and even say 'Could you just confirm that by email please, I am sure we will be engaging you'.

Before you do actually engage your accountant you still have the upper hand. Use it now because once you have signed it will be too late.

A TYPICAL BILL

When you buy items in a shop or supplier you usually get a bill with a full breakdown. You can see what you bought, how much that item cost and double check it if you wish. That's what we are used to.

Accountants don't generally send a breakdown with the bill even though it is made up of component parts of time. So much on calls, so much on accounts and so much on tax, say. So why do you just get a bill saying 'Professional services £2,520'? The answer is that more information on the bill simply generates queries that your accountant does not welcome. Like 'Is that what he is charging me for telephone calls? I only called a couple of times.' Clients do not generally appreciate how the time is costed so it will follow that they home in on the part of the bill that they feel is too much.

As we know, when we look at any bill our eyebrows can raise. So it is inevitable that, through lack of understanding of the charging basis, queries will follow.

Accountants (and lawyers) avoid this by just not putting in the details and retaining an air of mystery.

An example of a bill using the *small firm* rates in the table might breakdown as follows:

Junior – Balancing and summarising – 2 days	210
Senior – Check, make into final accounts – 2 hrs	70
Partner – Telephone calls over the year – 2 hrs	300
Partner – Review of accounts and tax – ½ hr	75
Partner – Meeting with you – 1½ hrs	225
TOTAL BILL FOR YOUR ACCOUNTS AND TAX **£880**	

So, out of the bill of £880, your accountant partner, who did no real number-crunching on your accounts, takes up a full £600 of it. That is 68% of your bill for about 25% of the time. Half of that was on your phone calls (chats and pleasantries) over the year.

So it is your partner's time that takes up the major part of the bill. He plays that down with the absence of a breakdown.

REVOLUTION

Many professions in recent years have become subject to fees pressure. Solicitors' fees dropped when the door to conveyancing was opened to non-solicitors. Opticians' charges collapsed when new business models like *Specsavers* marched in. Accountants suffered when the audit requirement for small companies was dropped allowing the unqualified guys to surge in onto that uneven playing field.

With the e-business and the growth in non-qualified firms offering the same services to smaller businesses at lower prices, the regulated sector of small firms (Chartered and Certified Accountants) had to adjust to compete. They could still make a good profit even charging half the amount they previously charged, so fees came down. Some firms still exist on the old system and these tend to be the larger partnerships, who impose high charges on their audit and other services. There can be little justification in charging £80 per hour for a trainee to basically act as a runner when the national minimum wage is about £7, but they can stick it on the bill and get away with it.

Some smaller firms carry on in the old way. They operate a strict time basis and don't like fixed fees. Whatever business you are running, professional fees have to be watched and, like any other cost, got as low as possible, without detriment to the quality of service you receive.

FIXED FEES

In the last 20 years the fixed fees arrangement has become more popular. Back in the 1980s, fixed fees were frowned upon by chartered accountants as not being 'professional'. How could you do a proper job or give the right amount of time to the work for a fixed fee? Times change, and with them attitudes to professional fees.

It is important to understand the difference between estimates, quotations and fixed fees. These words can be used cleverly and often qualified to disguise what they really are.

When you are given a price, look at the conditions on which it is given. Is it fixed or an estimate? Are there get-out clauses? There is often a clause following a fee quote, that says this will be confirmed when we receive your books and records. This may be a fair deal because records that are in a mess will obviously take more time to work on.

We are all familiar with comparison websites. The website *www.choose-an-accountant.co.uk* tell you they will provide a number of quotes from accountants so you can choose the best. Such sites are useful for other types of service: *www.check-a-trade.com*, for instance, has a roster of builders, plumbers, carpenters etc. They show photos of their work and have many testimonials from clients. Comparison sites do not work well for accountancy services. You cannot show 'satisfactory work', just opinions – always glowing.

I tested the accountancy site above and pretty well all the quotations were from non-regulated accountants. There were one or two testimonials clearly put there just for the sake of it that were meaningless. The names after the quotations were vague. Things like *'John, Leeds'*, quite impossible to check.

Initial accountancy price quotes are misleading. They lure you into thinking that this is a product like insurance, where you can make a reasonable judgement on price. You might feel you can compare charge-out rates. But in small firms these are vague, variable and arbitrary. As a partner, some clients would be charged £50 an hour and some £200.

What a quote from an accountant does tell you is the level at which that accountant sees himself. For a start, is he paying to be on such a site because he lacks work? Is he expecting to win a client on price? Is he making generic, meaningless claims about his ability? Is he making much of a second-tier accountancy qualification? Remember, these accountants are paying up front in some way to the site for the chance to quote alongside many others, so may say anything for new business.

The fixed fee will come in written form and should clearly state what it covers, what extras are 'thrown in' and what it does not cover. Then it is a fixed fee and not an estimate or a quote.

The main advantage of fixed fees is that you know what you are going to pay and you get an all-inclusive service. There is nothing like that all-inclusive holiday where you never have to think of your wallet. Some clients feel that paying a fixed amount by monthly standing order gives them security. Many of the national franchises use this system as they tend to have only the smaller-fee clients, and this approach can cover all their clients. All-inclusive deals, like holidays, have winners and losers. The trouble is, only the accountant will know for sure who's won and who's lost because he can monitor his time cost against the fixed fee. The client only guesses.

You do not know whether you end up paying more or less because of the fixed fee. If the accountant quotes a fixed fee based on what you tell him and then things turn out to be more complicated, he may look to cut corners. That could cost you in tax or in other ways; but the problem is that you will most likely be none the wiser if he does so.

With time-based fees you do give your accountant the best environment to do the most efficient work for you in fee terms. The disadvantage is the 'blank cheque' approach. This can be mitigated by getting him to give you an estimate of the cost based on the nature of your particular situation. This will be qualified as an 'estimate only', allowing the accountant to charge for extras, unforeseen events or if you are just unlucky with the tax man.

Generally the accountant will try to stick to his estimate, **especially if it is put in writing**.

CONTIGENT FEES

Sometimes fees can be neither on a time basis nor fixed. They can be dependent on outcomes. We are all used to these with estate agents. Contingent fees are now considered appropriate in certain circumstances. However, there are certain situations where they just won't work. For example, if you say, 'I will only pay you if my accounts are agreed by the taxman', you might find that you are shown the door.

You might be offered a contingent fee in association with a tax-planning scheme. This seems a good idea because it means you only pay when they save you money. For example, they say they will charge 10% of however much tax is saved by their work, *only if* they are successful. A swish accountant might already know the outcome, or be 90% certain. He knows that he will get his 10% and the client will be happy. So it's not really contingent at all – it's just a clever way to manage client expectations.

If you think you are due a refund and say to your accountant you will only pay if you get one, he will be able to make a quick assessment of your affairs and will know straight away if you are due one, so he can then agree to these terms. Usually those situations are quite simple, so he can quickly make that assessment and you producing vouchers or certificates of deduction will be like money in the bank. This work can be very profitable for accountants with very little hassle. It is a simple job that can be done quickly and a premium charged, because the client feels no loss in payment. Again, the client is very happy and has not felt the paying of a fee; it's just part of his tax.

CONTINUITY

Do remember that accountancy services generally roll on from year to year and for things to work to your best advantage it must be a mutually beneficial relationship. Getting 'one over' is not for the best. Getting that all-inclusive where you have really used the firm's services all the time will not be sustainable.

Paying a fair fee for an excellent service is the name of the game. If you try to push down a fee quote or play off one accountant against another you might end up with a quote that won't hold up, resulting in it being revised, or the service being cut, or even excuses thought up to vary the terms. Be careful with fixed fee get-outs.

WHAT ARE YOU PAYING FOR?

Earlier we saw that the cliché *'you get what you pay for'* does not necessarily apply... and while that may be right for *advice*, it isn't quite so when it comes to *service*.

A public house is legally obliged to display the price of a pint of beer. But in accountancy firms (and lawyers' practices, for that matter) you will see no sign of costs. Even at the first meeting, fees will not be top of the agenda. Details will come eventually but if you want them early you usually have to ask. In conjunction with your formal instruction letter, the phrase 'fees will be charged on the basis of the time and value of the work done' will usually be included somewhere in your letter of engagement, unless it is a pure fixed fee. Partner and staff rates per hour should be given.

Regulated accountants' governing body rules state that they must set out the basis of their charges, in writing, to new clients. If they fail to do this they can be censured and fined. So they comply, but the fee basis is set out in professional jargon and lies deep in that engagement letter. The unregulated accountants are by contrast more up front with their fees – charging, say, £100 per month plus VAT. Simple, understandable and clients like it.

Accountancy is not the most price-sensitive service. Charges year on year tend to be on a mutually understood basis. If you have a regular cleaner, gardener or even a banker that you use on a regular basis, you tend to agree charges at the beginning and then forget about them. This is where the accountant has the upper hand. His letter of engagement, as we have seen, will set out the basis of his charges and the best ones give the current hourly rates. This letter will usually provide for these to be increased at 6- or 12-month intervals. This effectively means that they can increase them each year as they see fit. What tends to happen is that clients accept this until a bill comes that seems larger than they would like or expect. They then have few choices – complain, leave or refuse to pay it.

Generally, if an accountant sees that by giving extra service more fees will be generated, he will go out of his way to do just that. There can be two extremes of clients: the one who penny-pinches and the one who pays a premium. Traditionally, accountancy is not a one-size-fits-all service and it will be tailored to the client's needs. Accountants will travel hundreds of miles just to get a signature on a document for one client but won't pick up the phone to take a call from another. How can there be such a difference? It is not personality – it is simply *fees*.

You might say, 'Surely they should all give the same service?' but accountants are human too. The huge mis-selling scandals in the financial services sector are all related to one thing – maximisation of profit. They did it by hidden commissions. Why? Because they were human, had mortgages to pay and families to support – just the same as your friendly accountant has.

You do not want your accountant on the back foot with time and costs. He might be receiving hidden messages from his client about his charges. Good advice can take up extra time, and if you don't have that available within your fee you are probably not going to get the best advice. Pressure on fees (competition) is good in one way but not when it comes to advice.

If you said, 'I don't care what I pay. I just want a five-star service, all possible reports and everything done in advance,' your accountant might feel he needs to assign a permanent member of staff to you, to get all technical aspects of your affairs checked and double-checked, hire specialist barristers for complex issues, engage extra temporary staff at your year end to get things done in the first few weeks, and take bank managers and financial advisors to lunch – all the time making sure you are kept fully in the loop about everything financial. It is all possible with available funds. Your service would be brilliant, but your bills astronomical.

THE BLINK TEST

A senior accountant once told me the fee procedure he might apply to clients who wanted a fixed fee:

> The client asks how much it is going to cost. The accountant says, 'Well, there are the basic accounts – that's about £750; then of course you will need a personal tax return and a business tax return – that's about another £500.
>
> We will be bringing in your wife as a partner, which will save you £1,000s in tax; her tax returns adds about another £400. So that's £1,650. Then we should allow for tax planning for next year, say £450, which takes us to £2,000.'
>
> At this point the client blinks furiously and you know you have reached the limit. So the accountant winds it up with the fixed fee at £2,000 and adds, 'We will include all telephone calls and meetings'.

The client has been dragged to his maximum but feels he is getting a gold-plated service. Has he been overcharged?

8

OVERCHARGING

Apart from that fixed unambiguous quote, the control over fees lies very much in the accountants' hands. They have the upper hand whether on the high street, in back upstairs rooms or in large partnerships.

Letters of engagement quote hourly rates which may seem to the untrained eye, unbelievably high. You, the potential client, have little means of comparison or 'shopping around' – you are presented with the hourly rate in a letter or in a meeting and have no way of knowing how many of these costly hours are going to be expended on your affairs. Fees are purported to be spelled out when in fact you are in the dark.

One thing we can say for the non-qualified or the unregulated is that they usually have their charges clearly laid out and in many cases paid monthly on a fixed basis. This is the franchise model and they have learnt and capitalised on the professions obfuscation on the subject of fees.

WHY OVERCHARGE?

Accountants will overcharge for various reasons:

- Human nature – the accountant wants to maximise profits

- To make up for the clients who create losses
- Because he knows he can get away with it
- Because it falls short of actual fraud
- Because it covers the cost of extras
- Because he sees you as 'a third party' to exploit

There are excessive fees that can be *got away with*, willing and unknowledgeable clients to *exploit*, all legal. So, given the situation any client should be on his guard. How do you compare? How do you know? Who can you trust?

JOBSWORTH

There are some 'jobsworths' in every field, and accountancy is no exception. It is rare, though, as generally there is plenty of work to do and to go round. So the jobsworth's mantra of creating work for the sake of charging for it is pretty rare. But watch out for:

1. Needless documentation
2. Over auditing
3. Management consultants
4. Management accounts not used
5. Financial life plans
6. Balance sheets for sole traders who are not VAT registered

IT'S SO EASY

Take a small-to-medium type firm. This is what can happen behind the scenes:

Say a client's accounts and tax return are taken to the partner for final approval. He looks at it for about half an hour and says it all looks fine – 'What was your time on this job?' he asks his accounts clerk, 'have we got the time ledger?'

The clerk says, 'The time ledger has not been updated and Shelia is away but I spent three hours on this job.'

'OK,' says the partner, 'I had a few calls with them in the year – that's two hours of my time max – plus today, that makes about £300, plus your three hours, plus one for finishing. What's your rate?'

'£80' says the clerk.

'So that's £320, making a total of £620 in time on this job. What did we charge them last year?'

'£1,250' says the clerk.

'Well, we can't lower that,' says the partner, 'he will expect it every year. We will make it £1,100 and tell him things were easier this year. He will be pleased at the reduction but it's not so much that we can't put it up next year.'

The accountant is pleased he has been able to charge more than the time costs. The fact is that the accountant has overcharged for the work done for that year.

When the client gets his bill he is pleased it's a couple of hundred less than last year. The accountant complimented him on his records in his letter. The client rejoices that he has a good accountant he trusts. He knows accountants can charge heavily but he's got a good one who will charge properly.

Not quite. He's got a good one all right – a very good one who knows how to make a profit hand-in-hand with getting a satisfied customer. Brilliant, in fact.

YOUR OWN WORST ENEMY

One of the worst questions you could ask your accountant is: 'I'm sure I sent you a letter a few years ago that had the date I moved into my new house – could you look it out for me?'

Instead of saying 'I'm not your welfare officer' he will be incredibly polite and say: 'Of course, I will get one of my staff to go through your file and find it.' (That might cost you an extra £150 on the bill.)

He then might say: 'Would you like it this afternoon? We can scan it and email it to you.'

You say: 'Oh yes, that's awesome – it's really urgent, I appreciate that.'

Accountant shouts to staff: '*Make that £350 extra on the bill.*'

Accountants, if they can, will charge more to clients that take what they perceive as 'advantages'.

When I was a trainee, I was helping out a friend who had a publishing company in London that employed about 20 staff. I prepared the books for audit by a medium-sized firm. Then I had a call with the senior partner in charge of the audit and I asked who he was sending to do my friend's audit this year. I remember clearly his reply: 'One man and his dog.' The 'dog' referred to a trainee who would get charged out to the client at about three times what the partner paid his secretary.

I had a friend who trained with the now defunct *Arthur Andersen* (formerly one of the Big Four). He said he spent much of the first year photocopying and he was charged out to the audit clients at the rate of a partner in a small firm.

PERCEPTION

There is, unsurprisingly, a general perception that accountants do charge too much for what they do. Accountants will disagree – mainly on the basis that they are 'worth it'. However, we only have to look at the letter of

114

engagement, described in detail in chapter 6, to see the scope for overcharging to occur. This sets the scene for accountants to squeeze the maximum benefit from the contract.

Huge fees by the Big Four and the taking of massive commissions on 'tax schemes' have hit the headlines in years past. But what about the small and medium-sized firms of accountants? You do not hear any headlines about their fees so the way is clear for them to basically charge what they like if they can get away with it.

What you find is that charges will vary widely. Logically it follows, then, that some are overcharging. The work is essentially the same so why do some firms charge 100% more? It's the *Mercedes* comparison again. You will pay 100% more for a *Mercedes* over a *Ford* quite happily, but do you want to pay 100% more for a *Ford* from another garage in the next street. Of course not, that's plain ridiculous and would never happen, but accountants are getting away with it.

In 2013 I called around a number of firms as a one-man company with an annual turnover of £200,000 and a profit of £50,000. Typical charges quoted for the end of year accounts and tax work were as follows:

Big Four	Difficult to pin down
Next 50	£2,000 – £2,500
Regulated small	£1,250 – £2,000
Non-regulated	£750 – £1,000
Franchises	£1,250 – £1,500

As you can see, they vary from £750 to £2,500, over three times as much. One of the Big Four was offering a 'remote' service where the price falls into the 'next 50' range.

There is no standardisation and an absence of fair competition, free markets and meaningful comparisons. The recommendation effect fuels this even more as you move away from price comparisons. And, as we saw, with accountants, price comparisons do not work very well anyway.

The financial services industry was given a big shake-up on charges in the last decade. Commissions had to be declared, then years later commissions got 'abolished'. But the industry got round it, charges became hidden again by some and still are. Accountants have faced some challenges on fees at the lower end with the competition from the 'non-qualifieds'. But as you move up the regulated firms then charges become more fluid.

Overcharging means 'billing an unfair fee for the work done'. Don't think this is the sole prerogative of accountants. It is business practice the world over and most will get away with it if they can. Go to a market in Morocco and ask how much that kaftan is. The first price can be inflated by 1,000%.

In the arena of professional services in this country, however, legislation and transparency supposedly make such practices difficult to get away with. Even so, accountants and their system can too easily get away with it.

LACK OF ACCOUNTABILITY

Overcharging generally goes unnoticed. Clients put up with it, maybe move on, but rarely complain. This lack of accountability means that overcharging can carry on.

A PLC company on the AIM market consulted with me. Having been charged £150,000 by a Top 50 firm for his audit, he then changed to another Top 50 firm who charged £48,000 for the same work. The client felt cheated by the first firm, but nothing came of it: no loss of reputation for the audit firm, no request for money back, just a client moving on. There is no retribution on the brand, no accountability. They know that there is an inbuilt confidentiality. The client is not going to go on the internet forum and say he had been a bit of an idiot when he wants to keep the reputation of his company.

The small businessman is generally a pragmatist. He will not complain for the sake of it or for moral reasons. No, he will generally put it down to experience and move on. Such good news for the accountant. Sting them for a few years then let them move on.

A disgruntled client might say 'I am going to complain to the *Institute of Chartered Accountants*, your governing and regulated body.' So they contact them. Shall I tell you their standard reply? – '*We do not get involved in fee disputes.*' This was the line for many years and still is officially. However, realising this was not quite fair – or good PR – they set up a mediation process where an official will look at both sides and try to reach an agreement.

Perhaps a more independent voice is needed. Like *Ofwat* or the *Financial Ombudsman*, where you send in evidence and they make a judgement.

COMPLAINING

Internet forums are full of clients complaining about charges. There is always one overriding question: Am I being overcharged or not? They just don't know because they can't evaluate it. They try desperately to do so but just end up with individual subjective judgements. Many comments flow in from other accountants – some agreeing, others saying you can't judge on a superficial assessment. Others try to pitch for the business, saying they can do it for half the price.

You might look at a bill for accounts and tax for the year of £2,000 and think 'that's expensive others are doing it for a third of the price'. What is not stated is that you had a number of meetings with your accountant, numerous email queries *you* generated, and some detailed telephone calls. All this was extra to the normal compliance work. The reality was that you had been undercharged and if the accountant had costed all his hours he would have been only getting £20 an hour instead of the norm of £120.

The problem is it is not easy to broach the subject with your accountant. If you go out for a meal and the bill seems too much you can query it. You will be given a breakdown on each item of food, drinks and service. They might even make a gesture and you may well go back to that restaurant. Querying your bill with your accountant is not the same. Accountants can seem innocuous souls but when it comes to bills they are razor sharp. Your query will be seen as something that could be done without. Most clients don't query bills, so why are you? You can be classed as 'trouble' and that is not good. Knowing how your accountant can twist the knife in your affairs makes this a daunting approach. You would not query the dentist's charges just before he puts his drill into your mouth. So how do you feel about querying your accountant's charges when you depend on him to do the best for you financially?

Often it's the last straw and once you query then it's the end. See what happened to one guy who posted this on a chat forum:

I queried my accountant on the 27th May, and only received a response this week. The response was via e-mail and basically said that 13 hours had been spent on my affairs doing XYZ. It did not include an hour by hour breakdown of who had carried out what, which is what I was after. I wrote back saying that a couple of items were not carried out with the attention to detail that I would expect from a firm charging on average £116.00 per hour. The response I received was slightly more brusque – pushing the blame for the mistakes over on to other organisations and admitting zero fault for anything. No apologies – a real take it or leave it e-mail.

So by this time I'm starting to get a little wound up. Getting shafted is hard for me to accept so getting shafted and being told to like it or lump it doesn't sit well with me. I wrote back outlining why I have queried the bill and tell the chap (who is a partner) that I don't feel their firm wishes to work with a company as small as ours, so therefore could I please have my documentation prepared for me to collect. Additionally I want a copy of their timesheets, and only then will I submit payment of the invoice I'm disputing. Guess what I've received back? Absolutely nothing. Nada. Zilch. And I'm shocked. I've told this firm that I'm leaving, taking my business with me, and I'm never going to use or recommend the firm again and they have confirmed what I thought all along, they just don't give a damn.

So, as we can, see the accountants hold all the trump cards. Namely, the client is just one of many – he can go or stay it makes little difference. The client's affairs are BIG to himself and of negligible importance to the accountant. Moving is a major move for client, nothing for the accountant. The client is in a stuffed position. The playing field is not level; in fact the poor client does not even have goal posts, just a stick to kick at.

The client just goes like the many others. Some accountants have a stream of clients leaving. Often those accountants seem great at first. But it's because they are great sellers. Things then come home to roost and you are lucky if you find out before the years have taken their toll.

My advice to this poor client is the theme of this book. Find the right type of accountant, then build up the right relationship so that they *do* give a damn.

JUDGING YOUR LEVEL OF FEES

In the first firm I worked for, the senior partner went out and bought a Rolls Royce and parked it in the firm's car park. He had to get rid of it because clients made comments – they felt that, if he could afford a Rolls, then they were being overcharged.

Your gut feeling that you are being overcharged will be almost impossible to change. But how can we judge? There is no yardstick. Unless you go and get your tax affairs or accounts re-done by another accountant, you have no independent method of ascertaining the correct charge. Ways around this are the increasing practice of fixed quotes, or a clear system of time recording delivered to the client. Fixed quotes are fairly common now but the automatic setting-out of the breakdown of time is not.

If you are not on a fixed quote then the best you can do is have a complete time breakdown with each bill. Some firms do this but it is rare. The ideal bill would have the time units, the staff member, their charge-out rate and a short description of the work done. I would like to see this mandatory – one day, perhaps.

You can try asking. It's not a bad thing to say at the first prospective meeting. But try and say it as a matter of course, not something you are specially requesting as you are unhappy. Remember, fees are not the favourite talking point of most accountants.

HOW DO I KNOW?

So how do you know if you are being overcharged? It is difficult but let's look for some light-hearted signs; not all these indicate an 'overcharge' some may just lead to large reasonable fees:

1. Glamorous reception
2. Receptionist does not seem to do much
3. Really nice coffee
4. Partner keeps you waiting
5. Partner has assistant with him 'taking notes'
6. No quote given
7. Vague fee references
8. Fees not mentioned at all, you had to ask
9. Partner suggests lunch but does not say 'no charge for his time'
10. Partner knows you were recommended
11. Excessive praising of their own abilities or work
12. Random phone calls suggesting things you are not too sure about
13. Sudden big bills
14. Lots of bills for little things

COMBINATION

So, if we were to pick a system that would indicate a fair approach to charging, then the ideal would be a combination of fixed and variable. My firm have tried to pioneer this and an example of our engagement letter is given at the end of this chapter.

The compliance work (the standard stuff everybody has to have) can be estimated reasonably accurately by any experienced accountant. A fixed price should be given. Times have changed, internet and comparisons abound.

If an accountant will not give a fixed price for this sort of work after analysing your details it's a bad sign indeed.

There will be variable charges, 'extras' that crop up due to clients' changes, external factors, business conditions, HMRC, VAT Investigations etc.

So it should be made clear how these apply.

AVOIDING OVERCHARGING

Let's look at five things that can help:

1. Get fees sorted at the start

Make sure you get more than the loaded letter of engagement. You want more than this *in writing*. Send an email paraphrasing what was said at the first meeting or reply to the letter of engagement with clarifications. Doing this before any work is done is good as it subconsciously enters the psyche of your accountant that you are careful about fees. Look for a fixed quote for compliance work or try and get something in an email.

2. Become a favoured client

Much has been said about how to become one throughout this book. He should not overcharge his family or favoured clients.

3. Create trust

Trust works both ways. Make sure you do your bit. Do not be untrustworthy to him. Stick to what you said about giving information. Be truthful. Keep prompt.

4. Choose the right firm

Get one the right size. Choose one that does not appear lavish with its surroundings. Choose one with similar size clients.

5. Mention fee levels occasionally

Even if you did this at the start, occasionally make a comment. For example when you pay the bill (by return – as I advise throughout) include a short handwritten note saying:

> Cheque enclosed, many thanks for your work, if I need to do anything extra to help keep charges at bay please let me know. Best regards.   John

While this may seem just a throwaway comment its effect is quite subtle. Your accountant will not in the least want to set out what you can do to lower charges. Hence he is unlikely to make a positive response to you. However, a mental note will have be made by him (and accountants are very good at mental notes) that you *do care* about the quantum of his charges.

This is the effect you want – that you are more than pleased with the way he handles things and will always pay, but do have due care and concern about the level of fees.

PICKING A PLUM

If we were to ask author *Owen Jones* who the bad guys were, the Big Four would come near top of his list. In his book *The Establishment: and How They Get Away With It* (2014), he devotes many pages to exposing how they help draw up the tax laws, then make millions out of trying to circumvent them for their clients. He is absolutely right; they represent the side of capitalism that nurtures the bad guys. Just like the financial advisors driven by commission into mis-selling, the Big Four are driven by human instinct to exploit the system for their own gain.

Yet these are the *good accountants* that have been portrayed by the media, the ones they turn to for quotes – for example, on tax changes. They are the face of accountancy that the public sees, the names that are known. So it's understandable that someone might go to one of these good accountants for their accountancy service, thinking they were getting the best.

So, posing as a potential client, I asked for a quote from one of the Big Four, for the year's end work for a small company. Below are the emails that followed:

1. **Email enquiry sent by me on the firm's website reply box:** I asked for their charge-out rates for me being a client.
2. **Their reply:** I have been handed your enquiry by the central website team. We do not have fixed charge-out rates for services, as this will depend on a number of factors, including the type and complexity of the work involved – for example, if this is an advisory or compliance project. It may be helpful for us to have a better idea of the services you might be interested in and some background, as I may be able to give you a better feel for the level of fees. Please let me know if this would be helpful. Kind regards. xxxx
3. **My response:** Many thanks. I have a small limited company and I need the first year accounts doing. The turnover is £200,000 and the net profit is about £50,000. I have kept records on spreadsheets and done my quarterly VAT. I need the year-end accounts doing (the deadline is about five months away), corporation tax and company secretarial. Can you give an indication of a cost for that please, or how you may calculate your charge. Many thanks. Chris Thomas.
4. **No response, so further email 12 days later:** Hi xxxx, I did email you back some details on 21st – did

you get these? Are you able to give a quote or charge out rates? Chris Thomas.

5. **Big Four reply:** Dear Chris, Apologies for the delay in replying – I have been out of the office. Please can you re-send your email of 21st August as I don't appear to have received it – it may have been blocked by our email filters. I will try to get back to you as soon as possible on receipt. Kind regards xxxx.

6. **My response:** This was it. Many thanks. I have a small limited company and I need the first year accounts doing. The turnover is £200,000 and the net profit is about £50,000. I have kept records on spreadsheets and done my quarterly VAT. I need the year end accounts doing (the deadline is about five months away), corporation tax and company secretarial. Can you give an indication of a cost for that please or how you may calculate your charge. Many thanks. Chris Thomas.

7. **No response, so my further email seven days later:** Hi xxxx, I am not sure whether you got my email of 9 Sept in response to yours of 8 Sept as you said you have spam filters that may block mine (I don't know why). Here it is again, if you are able to offer anything. Regards. Many thanks. 'I have a small limited company and I need the first year accounts doing. The turnover is £200,000 and the net profit is about £50,000. I have kept records on spreadsheets and done my quarterly VAT. I need the year end accounts doing (the deadline is about 5 months away), corporation tax and company secretarial. Can you give an indication of a cost for that please or how you may calculate your charge. Many thanks. Chris Thomas.'

8. **Big Four reply:** Hi Chris, I did receive this and your query has been passed on to my colleague in our

Entrepreneurial Business team, as I work in personal tax and this is not my area of expertise! She will be emailing you back with an indicative quote. Kind regards. xxxx

So after eight pointless emails, finally this ninth email arrived two months after my first request (**my comments are inserted in bold**). It is humorous to note that they have an Entrepreneurial Business team... Is that designed to make me feel I'm some sort of important innovator?

Dear Chris,

By way of introduction, my name is xxxxxx and I work in Private Company Services Tax in the London Office.

I believe you submitted the following query through our website:

It was not to the website it was via xxxx. It seems the Entrepreneurial Business team has been disbanded and is now called Private Company Services Tax.

'I have a small limited company and I need the first year accounts doing. The turnover is £200,000 and the net profit is about £50,000. I have keep records on spreadsheets and done my quarterly VAT. I need the year end accounts doing (the deadline is about 5 months away), corporation tax and company secretarial. Can you give an indication of a cost for that please or how you may calculate your charge. Many thanks. Chris Thomas.'

I have obtained quotes for this work based on the information that you have provided, however please note that these are approximate as we would need to take you on as a client formally and then assess your company's circumstances more fully before providing a formal quote.

So, finally we are getting a quote, or so it seems. The trouble is they are heavily qualifying it by saying it is approximate and that I have to become a client before they can give a formal quote.

This means, I would have to sign a letter of engagement agreeing to their time charges before they can give a quote that they have to stick to. All this, despite the fact, as we will see at the end, that they quote massively more than most other accountants. This firm wants total fee control over the poor client.

Statutory Accounts Preparation

If your company is a small company incorporated in the UK, then the fee for the preparation of the statutory accounts is £1,650–£2,000, with the range dependent upon the complexity of the accounts and the quality of the information provided.

Shouldn't accountants say whether a fee includes VAT or not? What they are doing is giving a quote that looks reasonable but then setting things up to pile on the extras.

Assumptions: To prepare the accounts we would need the period end trial balance (or period end books/records depending on what is kept)

We then prepare two drafts of the accounts; one pre audit/tax (if applicable) and one final version incorporating any audit/tax adjustments (if applicable)

We would also not be responsible for preparing the company tax disclosures

I told them it was on spreadsheets, which implies no trial balance is available. Why are they talking

about an audit? It would be obvious there is no audit involved. Am I supposed to know what 'company tax disclosures' are? Isn't that what my accountants are supposed to do or tell me?

Company Secretarial

The CoSec fees consist of a one-off charge of £500 for setup and an £850 annual fee for routine services.

Setup? A phone call and asking the secretary to get a file? So the first year's fees are £1,350 for filing one simple form online once a year that takes about 10 minutes. This is a ridiculous price. They are relying on my inability to know what is needed. This is bad.

Payroll Services

Please also find attached our quote for payroll services. Please note the following assumptions;

Set-up fee is based on APS contracting directly with the client. The attached fee proposal is based on no independence issues; There is no existing PAYE scheme in place; APS are required to facilitate payments; please note that we are only able to facilitate payments from a UK bank account to a UK bank account; We have assumed that the pay frequency is monthly; Payroll to be processed as a UK PAYE Scheme; All components are net to gross (with minor exceptions to be clearly identified); All employees are on local UK contracts; APS must be provided with the relevant information in an agreed format. We will operate NIC unless provided with a valid A1 / COC; Reporting requirement is based on standard star reports with no manipulation required.

Accounting & Payroll Solutions Group

Chris Thomas Payroll Compliance Quote

Section 1 Implementation

Data Collation and Computer Set-Up Our fees for data collection, set up on our in-house software, liaison with HM Revenue and Customs (HMRC)* and assisting with your Bacs registration (if applicable) will be in the region of £2,000 on the basis that the data provided is complete, accurate and in a format that enables us to complete the set up in an efficient manner. *For new employers, this includes registration with HMRC for a PAYE scheme and Deloitte as an agent; for existing employers, update HMRC records and re-register agent details. The set-up fee includes the provision of standard reports from our library and a basic accounting journal specific to your reporting needs. The design of other bespoke reports will be charged on a time-spent basis at an hourly rate of £250.

Section 2 Payroll administration and benefits reporting

Monthly Payroll Processing On the basis that the payroll processing requirements are reasonably straightforward, our fees for processing the payroll and issuing e-payslips will be £300 per month, plus £6 per employee. Our one-off fee for processing joiners and leavers will be £25 per employee added or removed after. Bacs Payments – from UK bank accounts only

Our fee for making the payment of net salaries, pensions, HM Revenue & Customs and other third party payments will be £25 per transaction run. Payments to UK accounts only. Payroll re-runs and Retrospective Adjustments Our fee for re-running the payroll at your request will be up to, but not exceeding, the monthly processing fee, dependent on the number of changes requested. Any retrospective adjustments required will be charged on a time spent basis according to the agreed hourly rates set out in Section 3 (Additional Work). The actual hourly rate applied will be dependent on the level of expertise required within our team to perform the work

Maternity calculations

Our fee for dealing with maternity pay calculations will be £50 per employee. Year-end returns – excluding Form P11D and PSA Our annual fees for dealing with the annual reconciliation, declaration and preparation of form P60 will be the equivalent to the monthly fee i.e. £300 plus £6 per P60.

Section 3 Additional work

Additional work associated with payroll compliance may be required or requested from time to time. In such circumstances, our fees for completing this work will be charged on a time spent basis at an hourly rate of between £135 and £500, dependent on the level of expertise required. Examples of the type of work would be the preparation of supplementary reports, backdated adjustments, notional termination calculations, remedial work on the initial transfer of the data and dealing with ad hoc enquiries and requests for information. July 2014, – Quote valid for a three month period

The above quote for payroll was quite confusing. It goes like this for one employee:

Set up	**2,000**
Monthly 12 x £306	**3,672**
Year end	**306**

First year total   £5,978

And the final bombshell – up to £500 per hour for extra compliance work. Compliance work is standard stuff. So if you had two hours extra work in the year to comply you could be looking at a total of nearly £7,000 for that first year bill for the director's payroll. That is over ten times what a payroll bureau would charge.

Corporation Tax Compliance

Based on the information that you have provided, we would estimate a cost of approximately £3,000 assuming that this would be a straightforward computation, and that there is no complicated ownership structure within the company. Please note that the above fee would exclude the following:

iXBRL conversion services;

Tax accounting work and preparation of tax disclosures;

Tax payments;

A review of potential withholding tax requirements and any associated filings (e.g. quarterly CT61 filings);

IFRS or FRS 101/102 advice work;

All other items typically excluded from our 'standard' compliance fee (i.e. R&D; detailed CFC work; WWDC, Transfer Pricing and Thin Capitalisation work; detailed Capital Allowances work etc.).

If you are interested in any of the above then please let me know or if you have any further questions then please do not hesitate to get in touch.

Many thanks,

Assistant Manager | Private Company Services Tax

WHAT HAVE THEY CHARGED?

After all that it comes out as £5,978 for the payroll and, with the previous accountancy work, making a total charge of nearly £12,000 for the year. There are provisions in the quote to increase the fee even more.

This compares with our other quotes averaging about £1,500 for all other firms. – so it works out at about <u>eight</u> times what others would charge for the same work. Is this a rip off? Are they *good* accountants?

A simple quote request appears to be going all round the houses, my affairs could turn into a farce like our comedian's did in that early chapter.

The client company is in for an appalling time. The Big Four accountants should have referred the client to a more suitable small firm, say, via the ICAEW. That would have been the *good* advice.

EXAMPLE ENGAGEMENT LETTER

Below I reproduce my firm's quote /engagement letter. The fixed price is £1,250. If we included payroll for one director that would be an extra £250. In total then for comparison that makes £1,500 all in as against the £12,000 the big firm was seeking to charge.

This example sets out clearly the services given and gives the client one all-inclusive fee. The fee, coming as it does from a regulated chartered firm, is highly competitive even with unregulated firms. This was for an actual client who was taken on in February 2015 and was typical of the small company service and price.

Dear Joe,

XXX PROMOTIONS LTD

Following on from our discussions I can now set out our services to you and how we can assist you in your business. Attached are our standard terms of business and client information. I also enclose HMRC form 64-8 for agents' authorisation. Could you please sign this HMRC form and return in the post with an original signature and the company name inserted.

Our Fixed Fee – what this covers

Having considered your circumstances and on the basis of our initial assessment and your representations we can offer the following services which will cover what us accountants call 'your compliance work':

I estimate that for the following services we would charge a fee in the range of £1,250 plus VAT. This a total price where you need no extras for the basic work and would be confirmed fully when we have all the year-end details for the preparation of the annual accounts. This price assumes that proper books and accounts are kept, balanced and summaries provided to us within six months of the year end.

For the fixed fee we would on the basis of the information given:

1. *Prepare Statutory Format Accounts for the company from the accounting records kept by you.*
2. *Certification of annual statements, turnover certificates or references as required.*
3. *Filing Financial Statements with Companies House.*
4. *Completion of all Corporation Tax computations, forms, claims for allowances and all normal annual correspondence with the Inland Revenue.*

5. Deal with Company Annual Return and company secretarial matters (provided we are supplied with on line filing code).
6. Deal with all money laundering formalities, HMRC matters, your file set up and information collation.
7. Give at no extra cost up to 5 time units of queries throughout the year. This can be emails, calls, references – those ad hoc matters should be taken care of in this.

VAT registration, wages and sub-contractors

You are responsible for these matters but we can advise, register your business, or operate your payroll.... On request.

Basic included tax planning

Included within your compliance work fee is a tax minimisation review conducted at the year end when we do the accounts designed to help your company pay your fair share of tax – but not a penny more! We regard this as part of our service to you.

If you also ask us to help you look at more complex tax saving options, or you need our help putting the simpler tax saving options into effect, then this will be charged on a time basis unless separate fees are agreed.

Tax Provisions

Tax will be paid in arrears and so you should make provision for these to be covered. We can advise if we have information about your income and expenses on what you should be putting aside on request.

Consultancy and advanced tax planning

If you require special meetings, serious tax planning, cashflow advice or in fact any assistance with business *matters then these fall as extras to be billed for as we go. Our standard terms will cover this work in the absence of fixed quotes and this will be charged for on a time basis.*

Guarantees and safeguards

The standards you should expect from us we take very seriously. We are a regulated firm and have to do ongoing education, money laundering and full insurance. If you are ever unhappy with any aspect of our work, we will without question respect your right to query our bill and reach a compromise. Please do not hesitate to contact us – we welcome feedback.

Extra Services

The fee quoted is the basic service for what we consider the minimum requirement of your company and tax minimisation. We can have meetings about tax planning, cash flow/budgets, helping you get more out of the business and make more money. These are extra services always available at your request. They will cost extra but we would aim to give 'value for money' in that there is a net saving in the end to you.

The aim of our firm is to provide a first class service, without charging an 'arm and a leg' from an experienced firm. It will include looking at ways to help you run your business, save you tax, and make your business as easy, enjoyable and as hassle-free as possible by keeping you in line with the legislation that affects your tax and accounts.

Our office

We keep our overheads as low as possible by using the best modern technology and software. Our reception and secretarial costs are much lower than other firms of Chartered Accountants and we believe your affairs are handled better too. We want you to recommend us to others so we do try very hard. Xxxxxxx FCA, my partner in the office will tend to deal with routine matters and my function is more of a consultancy. If you get any communications from HMRC or Companies House please forward them on to us if you are not sure what to do. If they are routine we will deal with them without bothering you further or, if necessary, contact you as required.

In the meantime, thank you for giving us the opportunity to be of assistance.

Best wishes

9

ADVICE

Most people love giving free advice, often when you don't need it or haven't asked for it. But we are talking about professional advice and this is offered purely on a financial basis. Forgive the cliché, but *there is no such thing as a free lunch* – especially with professionals.

Be aware that you will have to pay up for proper advice that will save you money – perhaps lots of it.

But even more important is that, to maximise the value of the advice for which you are paying, you should listen 100% to it and **act on it**.

GOOD ADVICE

So let's assume you are paying promptly and not incurring unnecessary extra charges; then what advice can you expect? Any of these could be judged as examples of 'good' advice:

- When an effective solution is found to a messy situation. You have fallen foul of legislation/filing/returns and instead of making a meal out of it your accountant points to a solution.
- When you are doing something wrong and it is explained for you. Your accountant makes a point of

explaining to you that this is not the correct way to go about things and shows you what to do.

- When your situation is analysed and a considered solution given. You are at a crossroads, there are a number of options with different outcomes. The pros and cons are investigated and conclusions offered.
- When your accountant is truly proactive, he can spot something in advance. For example you start selling small digital products in the EU and he tells you you need to register under the special VAT scheme that has no de-minimis limit.

These are just a few. Good advice is what you should expect if you have put the measures in place to get it. You have moved up from a 'third party client' to a **favoured client**. But *good* advice is particularly hard for a client to judge and particularly easy for an accountant to manipulate. Some accountants are masters at projecting themselves as purveyors of constant *good* advice when it's actually standard stuff.

I had a client who was always pleasant, funny and complimentary and, best of all, paid my bills without a query within a week of them being sent. We were examining a part of a personal services contract in his absence. I was in a professional boardroom with a good lawyer and his manager and we were brainstorming all the options. Our brains were working in overdrive, firing off each other. We all know those lacklustre meetings where everyone is holding back waiting for others, this was the opposite. The client had generated the goodwill in us all and we were working together. It was costing about £1,500 an hour and it took all morning. We eventually came up with the best option. That good advice from the lawyer and me cost over £6,000 for a morning's work but we knew the client would not quibble. The client and his manager received no paperwork from either of us and were just told to 'do this'.

It saved them £100,000. Our bills were immediately paid. The client had had the best service and advice possible, saving thousands.

STANDARD ADVICE

This is what would be expected of any responsible accountant based on the textbook response. However, this advice can be tinged with the 'no comeback' factor. Accountants don't want any retributions from you, the taxman or their professional body. They will therefore tailor their advice for this. You are not getting any extra in your advice, you are actually getting the minimum. If that's all you want, then fine; after all, the minimum is better than bad advice.

This **standard professional coverage** we have covered before is typical of the advice meted out by the big firm in our children's book publisher freelancers example in Chapter 4. There is no comeback from the taxman; the client thinks their advice is absolutely right. In our example, the big firm accountants can then charge a hefty fee for transferring all the employees over to PAYE and managing a scheme. It's a win for the accountancy firm, a win for the taxman, and a minus score for the client.

INADEQUATE ADVICE

Sadly, this is what some clients pay their accountant for. This advice falls below **standard professional coverage**. However, most of the time the low standards will go completely unnoticed by the client. It can be disguised or fudged and can amazingly also appear to be good advice.

I have come across a number of small clients who have been told to trade as limited companies when it was of no real benefit (in chapter 11 I list the pros and cons). However, it is of substantial benefit to the accountant, as he can double and even treble his fees, whereas a client's financial benefit is often negligible unless high profits are made.

You might need to be wary of this, say, if you were using a franchised, unqualified accountant and you were a 'third party' client. If the accountant's main motivation is his fees, we are getting very close to that old mis-selling that takes place when the financial incentive to the advisor overrides the 'best advice' that should be given.

Another example of inadequate advice might be where your accountant does your annual accounts and your turnover has risen to £75,000 – very close to the VAT limit. He does not mention that it looks like you will breach the registration threshold for VAT very soon and therefore need to register, so you miss it and end up with penalties. This is not technically challenging, it is basic stuff. Either your accountant has rushed your job out without a proper review, can't be bothered to tell you or completely missed it. Whichever way, you have received inadequate advice.

BAD ADVICE

If we take our VAT example above, bad advice would be where you had been over the limit for a few years and your accountant has said nothing to you each time he sent the annual accounts to you. You are then rumbled by the VAT man. You are the subject of a backdated VAT registration. This can be a very expensive affair. You are charged with paying over the VAT on all income even though you did not charge it to your customers. This could be say 20% of all earnings going back those years, and that's on gross earnings not profit.

So where does your accountant stand on this? Why has he not pointed this out to me? Surely he must take responsibility? You contact him and ask. He points out that in his letter of engagement to you it says quite clearly: '*We take no responsibility for VAT matters unless specifically requested. It is your duty to monitor your turnover to ensure compliance with regulations.'* You are stuffed.

Furthermore, you have now annoyed him with your accusations so he stiches you up without you knowing. The effect of your VAT payments is that all your income in the accounts going back years is overstated, meaning you have paid too much tax. You are entitled to make a backdated claim to reduce your profits and get a tax rebate. But, of course, hand-in-hand with his initial bad advice is his fear of any comeback on him for sending in tax returns that subsequently turn out to be wrong. So he does nothing and tells you nothing. You have paid more income tax than you should as well as the VAT and you think it's all your fault. He has been negligent but gets off scot-free.

So if you get the feeling that you have had bad advice be very careful about the explanations given. Change accountants and get a fresh look.

Also beware of advice which does not relate to your circumstances.

> *An accountant walked past a homeless man. 'Spare any change, guv?'*
>
> *The accountant says, 'Why should I?'*
>
> *The man says: 'Because I have no money for food.'*
>
> *'How does that compare with the last quarter?' retorts the accountant.*

SELLING ADVICE

Accountants are, by the nature of their relationship with you, in a charmed position when it comes to selling you 'extra' services. This can take on many forms – You need this software... Have you thought about a pension...? A limited company would be good for you... We should do your VAT, you keep getting it wrong... You can save thousands in tax with this scheme... Extra accountancy work – tax planning, inheritance tax reviews; management consultancy-like bookkeeping services, business plans, financial services and even taxman insurance protection... And so on. As you can see, there can be something to suit most clients. There is your valued and trusted accountant saying, with authority, you need one of these.

Accountants attend courses regularly to keep themselves updated. Most courses cover tax and auditing but some are specifically designed to increase the fees of the practice. One of the main ways they are told to do this is by getting more fees out of existing clients. This does not mean necessarily putting up prices, although you might be surprised to learn that some do tell you to do just that. The argument for that goes something like: if you put up prices by 10% the few that drop off will actually be lower than the 10% overall rise. This would not work for 'price-sensitive' businesses but the accountant–client relationship is generally not one of those. So it works for them.

However, their main way of getting more fees is by the accountancy practice selling more services to the existing client bank. The logic on this is simple and attractive.

Say your accountant has 100 clients with average fees of £1,000 each. That gives him a turnover of £100,000. If his overheads, that is rent, rates, staff costs and office costs are £60,000, then his profit is £40,000 per year. That is what he earns. Now say he sells 'extra services' to his client bank. The accountant sell extras and fees could go up by 50%. That is not that hard if he is providing extras that make sense to the client. Then look what this does to the profit. The fees are now £150,000, overheads increased by

£10,000 to £80,000. His net profit is now £80,000. He has doubled his 'salary'. Who is going to walk away from that?

So, faced with this incentive to 'sell', how does your accountant tackle it? Let's try and look at what type your accountant might be. Consider these basic types:

- An aggressive seller
- An opportunistic seller
- A laid-back seller
- An active non-seller

Have a think which category of these your accountant falls into ...

If he is at the top of the list, the accountant's ethical objectivity may have been compromised if he has moved from his normal work into the domain of a financial services commission-based salesman. So put your accountant into one of the four types above, then decide. For example, if your 'laid-back' accountant says you really need this, then you probably do. If your 'aggressive seller' accountant says you need this, you may not.

TAGGED-ON FINANCIAL SERVICES COMPANIES

Some accountants realised that financial services can be very well rewarded and, instead of passing this business on to others, set up their own firm of independent financial advisors alongside their accountancy practice. They would usually recruit a person – Mr Smart Suit, say – to specifically deal with enquires and more. Often this would be on a sort of partnership basis where 50%, say, of the commissions or fees came back to the partners of the firm, often by payment through a separate limited company of which they were directors alongside Mr Smart Suit.

Mr Smart Suit would have full access to the accountant's files and go through all the clients' personal details to see what extra financial products might be suitable or saleable. He would then contact the clients, explain his association and arrange a meeting. What a convenient arrangement and a great earner for the partners for doing little except finding an extra desk – and as a great bonus, it makes them look like they are being proactive accountants serving your interests.

Having said that, there can be a spin-off benefit to the client in using the accountants' own financial advisor rather than another unconnected one. Mr Smart Suit will not want to overstep the mark and the natural tendency towards selling unneeded financial products would in fact be tempered. But Mr Smart Suit still has to 'sell' to justify his existence. The very nature of the commission-driven system worked against the client's interests. Year after year of mis-selling legislation finally changed things in 2014. But despite the changes that came in in 2014 the system is still skewed. He still has to 'sell to earn', so that will come first, and 'best advice' will come second. While the commission system has moved on and is now replaced by a fee or percentage charge, there are still inherent motives in the system for the financial salesman to not offer 'best advice' all the time.

No financial advisor is going to say 'It all looks great this year, leave things alone, here's my 1% fee please.' No, he is going to move you around a bit to justify his 1%.

Should you just inherit £300,000, no financial advisor is going to say: 'Use that £300,000 you have just received it to pay off your mortgage. Our fee is 1% so give me £3,000 for telling you that please.' No he is going to tell you how with, careful management, that sum can be invested to give you an 8% return. Then his 1% seems insignificant. Some of the larger, more prestigious, financial firms have even been very clever at disguising percentages in so-called 'fund management fees'.

It's ironic, but the best person to advise you would actually have been your accountant. Now, unfortunately, a combination of the government and the FCA (formerly the FSA) have outlawed your accountant from telling you to pay off your mortgage, that you get no tax relief on, with the inheritance money you have just received. It's a criminal offence for him to give investment advice (unless he has extra qualifications). Sheer brilliance, don't you think? Only a financial advisor can tell you that. Trouble is these guys in smart suits have a love affair with investments, insurance and, their key word, **protection**. The idea of paying off your mortgage would make them shiver.

SUPER ADVICE

This is the advice that goes 'the extra mile', the advice most people want but don't get. Not advice that tells you how to do things illegally, or more specifically *evade* tax, but advice that is the best you could possibly have from a professional accountant. It might be how to *avoid* tax in a way that's not illegal – and nobody wants to pay more tax than necessary. There are grey areas in tax and an experienced accountant may tell you how you can exploit those without falling foul of the taxman.

In my earlier example of the difference between the advice of the small firm and the large firm, the advice given by the small firm to make some changes then stay self-employed was *good* advice. It would have been *super* advice if the partner had taken it a stage further and said: 'Here is a sample contract used by another client that you can use for your freelancers. I've altered it for you; get all your sub-contractors to sign it.' You have had *good* advice already and now he has put the icing on the cake and made it into *super* advice.

This advice is the crème de la crème and may be reserved for family, long-time clients or those with a special relationship. It won't usually be cost-based. Your relationship is key and has to be top-notch to get this extra level of advice. Remember, to get this you need to be that **favoured client.**

THE MILLION-DOLLAR QUESTION

Sometimes if you feel things are going round in circles and you are not getting that piece of advice which you need to resolve a situation, you need to come out and ask the question:

What would you do if you were me?

10

SERVICE

THE HONEYMOON PERIOD

When you first get your accountant, you feel relaxed that there is this new scrutiny of your affairs. You are relieved that the appointment you have made has solved one area of your financial and business life, and optimistic because you think you have chosen carefully or followed a good recommendation. Tax and business is going to work better now you have this professional alongside. You feel happy and reassured that your business or your finances are in good hands. It's all upside. With all this and *myside bias*, the relationship will start with a lift. Your accountant will be on a pedestal – at least for a short while.

As is natural, your accountant will 'sell' themselves to you, either at the initial meeting or afterwards, by making claims of what they can do. Promises of service can be made, so remember – or better, make some notes of – what was promised. Write down the essential points he makes. This might be useful to refer to later if the service falters. Contemporaneous notes are always good evidence (as lawyers will tell you) should you need to offer gentle reminders in the future. You should have that 'letter of engagement' which sets out what he will be doing for you but your notes will go into much more specific detail and can prove to be useful evidence in the future on top of the standard letter.

From the accountant's point of view he is eager to create a good first impression with his new client, so in that first period he will make sure he gives them the attention they want. A good accountant will have sized his client up and tailored his advice, time and attitude to be in rapport with his client. He can start on top form. He should have quickly assessed your needs and offered a solution.

At the start of the relationship there is usually a lot of goodwill. Keeping this goodwill is important, so keep up these pleasantries and courtesies that you first had in place. Don't let little things niggle you into treating him in an offhand manner. The goodwill is for your benefit, so look after it and try to prolong the honeymoon.

One accountant told me bluntly how the honeymoon period ends. At first the client is all over him, emailing, ringing him up saying his advice is fantastic. Then the accountant sends them a bill and they suddenly go quiet.

SERVICE YOU SEE

When you take your car in for a routine service and the reception area appears efficient – well laid out and you are booked in quickly and efficiently by an extremely pleasant guy behind the desk – you will feel a certain confidence that the car service will be done properly. You don't see anything about the actual service work but you are impressed by what you do see. When you pick up the car you are told about some things that will need doing soon, the car is washed with covers on the seats. Your confidence level is at 100%.

What you don't know is that, while they may have white-collar staff queuing up to sit behind a desk and give exemplary customer service, they cannot find any mechanics to actually get under the bonnets and get dirty. Trainees are set to work unsupervised and can leave in the middle of jobs. The car service gets botched but the car is always cleaned by volunteer workers for a free lunch. Or a garage may be in financial trouble so they don't bother changing the oil but charge for it. No one knows and it's only years later the damage sets in anyway. The car is always ready by 4pm with all those extras done as well. Remember, you don't see what goes on in the workshop. They know that it's what you see that counts, so they make that small percentage count. Accountants know this too.

THE ACCOUNTANTS' 5% RULE

With accountancy you won't generally be involved in the behind-the-scenes work. In fact many clients haven't got a clue what goes on here or how much time is used up. Clients see the offices, the smile of the reassuring partner and those beautifully presented accounts that come through in a big package after quite a long time (so assuming lots of good work was done) for them to sign off. The final product looks the business.

Accountants know the importance of this 5%. Get this right and set up the conditions for the *myside bias* effect. You can get away with a lot if your 5% holds up – anything from not admitting mistakes to talking the client into a tax avoidance scheme or carrying out work to generate fees.

During my training, I worked for five firms of chartered accountants. It was always drummed in that what the client saw had to be 100%. With the rest of the work you could take shortcuts, make estimates and just get by – but, above all, get the job out and billed without the possibility of comebacks either from the client or the tax man affecting the firm's general reputation and standing with HMRC. That was the general rule.

When the job concerned a partner's relative or friend then they would take a bit more interest in the work. They might come into the accounts preparation room and ask how it was going. Any issues coming out? Any queries? There was unusual attention for these clients – our **favoured clients**. When it came to a final review there would be much more interest, looking for tax savings, checking that the right amount of time was chalked up. With the non-favoured clients often the partner's interest would be negligible – if it looked okay on the surface then just get it out with a bill.

WHAT SHOULD BE EXPECTED?

Let's then look at some requisites of good service as they apply to our accountant:

1. Efficiency
2. Timeliness
3. Know you
4. Staff and specialists
5. Communication
6. Availability
7. Value
8. Statutory compliance

1. Efficiency

If you end up with an accountant who seems inefficient then you could be in for a rough ride. As accountancy is highly concerned with time, if your accountant has not got a grip on this you are in trouble. Does he seem to waste time? Do meetings or calls seem to go on a bit longer than necessary? Your accountant should be efficient with his time on you to the point of not being rude but occasionally seeming a bit short. He is then taking command and operating effectively. Time is king and should be managed 100%.

2. Timeliness

You would expect a level of promptness. If meetings are arranged then he should be on time. He should also prompt you regarding deadlines and tell you your tax in good time (providing you have given him ALL the information).

I was once recommended to a solicitor for a contentious matter. He was one of the senior partners. I had a 2pm appointment and he came back from lunch at about 2.30 with a colleague. As he passed me in reception he said a very polite hello and advised me his colleague was going to see me, not him as had been arranged. I felt a bit put out as the meeting had been arranged with him personally on recommendation. Anyway, I went into the meeting with his colleague, pumped him for advice and never instructed them.

3. Know you

As I've already said, to give good advice an accountant needs to know his client. Good service, then, is about asking the right questions to get to this position. You may wonder why it's relevant that your accountant wants to know where you go on your holidays, how many children you have, does your wife work, do you have a mortgage … You may think this is not about your business, but what your accountant is doing is learning to understand your circumstances so that when you ring up and say, for example, 'I need some short-term cash for the business', he can give you the best service by giving the right advice. It may be that the cheapest way is to raise it on your house mortgage and *because he knows your circumstances* he can advise on minimising the liability issue. Valued clients may get told the merits of having an offset mortgage, for others it may never be brought up. It is highly unlikely that an experienced accountant will ask you questions that do not have a bearing on his potential future work for you. He is not the taxman; he is on your side.

So ask yourself: does your accountant really know you? Do you get the feeling he can't remember you unless he reads the file? Do you get allocated the new kid on the block? In short, has he done that KYC we have talked about?

4. Staff and specialists

Having the right staff put onto to your work is getting the right service. When you have a computer accounts software issue you want someone with experience of that program to be solving it for you. Your accountant with his staff should be familiar with the main accounting software i.e. *Sage, QuickBooks, Xero.* Your main accountant is like a GP – he must identify issues and either propose a solution or refer.

There are a few times when specialists are needed. For example, a development project that has specialist VAT considerations. A general practitioner would not deal with this every day so he may call in a specialist and the client will be expected to pay. Other examples are complicated tax schemes, share buy-backs, employee share options. Your guy should be identifying your needs and making recommendations in an objective way. The trouble with the larger firms is they have here a conflict of interest. To recommend you for examination by another department in the firm is more profits for them, so beware. Where the specialist is external to the accountancy practice you can feel comfortable that you are getting objective advice and probably better service. Also, your accountant is likely only to have called in an external specialist if really necessary for your affairs.

5. Communication

You need to be able to communicate effectively with your accountant. If he is failing on this front you could be in real trouble. But this would be most unusual as pretty well all practitioners are fairly skilled communicators. The staff that can't communicate well get kept in the back room churning out the work.

Keep up the communication by not being a bore and listening attentively to what he says, keeping your dialogue to relevant questions not a diatribe about your lifestyle.

6. Availability

If you are an existing client and you ring up with a query, then if you do not get straight through to someone you should be called back either that day or the next. Email queries should be answered in two to three days. These are just guidelines, and exceptions occur, but longer might ring some alarm bells. The response you get should deal with your query or suggest a further course of action. If when you put down the phone you feel no wiser, or no nearer to resolving the issue, then that's not a good sign that you're getting the right service.

7. Value

There is a link between service and price. But what most want is value (for money). No one wants to feel 'ripped off'. But of course we are back to the old theme of 'how do you know?'

So real value would be *good service, low fees and done immediately*. Is that too much to expect? The short answer is yes. So have some patience. An accountant is already under time pressures to be fast, and no one likes to be put under more pressure that is not of their own making. He wants to be *accurate* but this competes with *fast*. He has many deadlines already – for tax, for Companies House and for staff. If you put him under time pressure because you have not been dutiful with your own affairs or left it late, it is not going to help.

8. Statutory compliance

You do not want to fall foul of regulations, tax deadlines and Companies House. Your accountant should be keeping you in line with this. So is the responsibility all his. Not surprisingly some clients think it is. No, his responsibility is just to tell you *once*. So a letter or email reminding you to supply something or respond is all that he has to do to discharge his responsibility. He takes the horse to water and that's it. If you are in any way dilatory it's your own fault. So the best advice here is treat all his requests seriously, as you may not get another warning. Super service would be further reminders, then a phone call. That could be the case for the **favoured client** but if you are not a close relative expect that to be reflected in your bill taking your dilatoriness to a compensation level of fees.

COMPLACENCY

After the flying start things should settle into a more routine system. Your accounts are due, you take your books in, you get your accounts to sign and are told your tax. You get a bill.

He may have assigned this routine work to his staff. If that seems to be working well he will move away from your affairs. This will save time costs, and give him more profit or maybe lessen your bill. That may be okay. You may find if you ring up with a query it will be dealt with well.

Your accountant's time may also be in strong demand with other clients and new clients can come along suddenly with immediate urgent problems to sort out. If you want more you are going to have to ask.

So, if you feel the need, you must move to a more proactive role with him. He is still *good*, just busy with others who maybe are more demanding. If you feel you are on his back burner, then send a polite letter to your accountant letting him know how you value his services and feel that you require a little more attention. You could suggest a meeting or lunch to discuss your current status and do a mini 'health check'. When writing do reassure him with some subtlety that you want to continue to use his 'most valued services'.

Remembering fees, at the end of the good lunch that you have paid for say 'Those were some good things you pointed out – if you need to send me a bill for this time please do.' You might get a pleasant answer.

CONFUSION

With so many clients to look after and details to remember, there is a professional syndrome where one client's detail may become confused with another. Something in your brain has linked the two clients and once this has happened it is quite difficult to unscramble. I had many clients with the same surnames and when you act for ten Joneses and two of them look and sound the same, your memory plays hell!

When an accountant says 'I need to check your file' it could mean: 'Hang on, I can't remember a damn thing about that.'

MEETINGS

Meetings with your accountant are expensive. They need to serve a purpose or could constitute overcharging. Meetings are a highly effective way for a professional to convey his professionalism to a client. If your accountant calls a meeting seemingly for the sake of it, then beware: it will just be a PR exercise. There may be a reason given but make sure you analyse whether this reason is valid to *you*. The meeting should be totally productive from your point of view – not necessarily what you want to hear, but instructive and constructive, advancing your affairs in some way.

On the flip side, never having a meeting is not necessarily a danger sign. You could be some distance away, or there are no issues with your affairs and any queries can be dealt with by phone or correspondence/email. Nor should you be alarmed if your accountant tends to put off your requests for meetings in favour of resolving your query in other ways. He may just be saving you costs. As meetings are expensive your accountant will be looking to recover all his time costs, including travel, from you in some way. If he thinks you cannot shoulder it he will try to avoid a meeting in favour of, say, a phone call.

Bearing the costs of a meeting in mind, your accountant should only agree to a meeting when there is a tricky point to be explained, an exchange of dialogue is needed, there is a difficult decision to be made – or you absolutely insist on one irrespective of the cost. By default, the 'chairman's' role is on him. He may use a prepared agenda or not, but in any event he should conduct the meeting efficiently and effectively and take notes.

Think about the feeling you have after the meeting. Was it worthwhile? Did you learn anything? Do you now have a plan to go ahead with? If it's left that parties will 'think about it', that may be a cop-out which just encourages procrastination and further costs. Effective meetings clarify grey areas, push things forward, draw conclusions, and end with a decision. This is all part of good service. You had the professional and the client together in the same room, technical points could have been covered before – you should have come to a decision and progressed.

YOUR MANTRA

Like the carpenters:

Never use a screw when a nail will do

Yours should be:

Never meet for advice when a call will suffice

BACK-ROOM ANTICS

The preparation of end of year accounts goes through a number of stages. Many people can work on your accounts production – from interns, trainees, secretaries and even the partner himself. This combined effort goes into producing a set of finished figures.

All those involved make decisions along the way on the figures they come across in your records. A junior has to interpret your handwriting or an abbreviated computer entry. The more senior staff may have to interpret your circumstances and make judgements. The question then develops: Are the right calls being made in my best interest? Is this behind-the-scenes work serving me well?

These tax-affecting judgements may be small things, like the junior staff deciding whether an expense is personal or business. But the big adjustments can come in the partner's final review: for example, where he spots that you have not paid out any wages to your wife who he knows helps in the business. Either way, you are subject to judgement calls all the way along, see-sawing your profits.

Staff can get up to tricks, making estimates and guesses, balancing write-offs and allocations of personal use, and even using cover-ups because they just can't get your books to balance. This will be fair game for those engaged on the work. Like anyone in business, they just want to get the job done with the minimum of hassle. So, instead of raising a query, they go for the easy route, allocate and move on. The decision as to whether to go one way or the other often depends on the client relationship. So be nice to the staff. Remember, if you are rude to your cleaner, you might get your bath washed with your face flannel and never know. If you are a pain to the accounts staff, when they come to allocating an unclear expense between personal or business they will undoubtedly go for the easy option and allocate it to personal, quite rightly doing so under the legitimate guise that it was 'unidentified'. Why should they put in the extra effort to determine exactly what it is and under what business heading it should properly fall to get tax relief? They will no doubt save that 'extra mile' for that nice gentle Mr Clarkson who is always so pleasant and gives them all a bottle of wine each Christmas.

Many years ago I worked on a well-known media group's accounts. We were the auditors. They had 50 companies in the group and they were all about three years in arrears with their audited accounts (this was before the days of Companies House fines). The policy had been to pay any bill out of any company in the group that had the money, irrespective of whose liability it actually was. This is an accountant's worst nightmare because when you do a set of company accounts you have to agree the inter-company balances. I put together a 50 by 50 matrix of all the balances to be agreed. We engaged a temp to specifically work at trying to agree them. A whole year down the line, with huge client's fees sent regularly on account, it just would not agree. It was out all over the place. Finally, after deliberating over one weekend, I came in and wrote the lot off with some journal entries in about an hour. Job done. The partner – my boss at the time – didn't want to know any details. Did the accounts balance? Yes, absolutely. 'Well done,' he said in so many words, 'let's move on then and get the final bill out' and promptly arranged a lunch with the MD. Only we knew that we had, in practical terms, wasted a year's work which had cost the client huge fees. Professionally, however, it may still have been right.

KNOWING YOUR TAX LIABILITY IN TIME

Clients often complain that they were not told their tax liability until just before it was due. The problem the accountant has is that all the work on accounts and the tax return has to be completed before he can calculate your tax. He will not want to give you a figure at the start, as it could turn out to be erroneous in the light of later work. He will only want to give you the tax figure when he is absolutely sure – and that is only possible at the end of all the work.

If you want to know your tax earlier then follow these simple rules:

1. Get your complete books and tax return information in to him early
2. Make sure you always pay his bill promptly
3. Answer any queries by return
4. Confirm with him when you will get the accounts

Sounds simple, but how many clients do all those? Not many – one or two is not enough. Some clients just do No. 2 and expect it all to be hunky-dory.

DO NOT DELAY

Ozzy and Sharon Osborne had a $1.7m charge filed against the family for unpaid taxes, and then more, taking it to over $2 million. Why, when they had money rolling in, could this happen, and what had their accountant done?

Well it turned out that *Sharon*, who did the finances, had failed to meet with her accountant to deal with these important matters. She recalled she had cancelled two meetings with him over the last 18 months because she was too busy. The lesson here is that your accountant can't work in the best way for you unless you work with him. He will take the horse to water and leave him there to drink or die. Could the *Osbornes* have been the opposite of his **favoured clients,** exasperating him and his staff? We do not know. Compensation could have been in the fees charged. Who knows?

The *Osbornes* might do the wrong things, going against what most of this book advises. But then those in the music business are often at that end of the scale. The fees compensate, so you see the net result. You ignore requests from your accountant at your peril. Don't expect a second reminder – unless you are that **favoured client** or a very high paying one.

To get good service you do have to take some responsibility for getting information to the accountant, otherwise you are lulling your accountant subconsciously into your bad habits. Your accountant will work better for you if he knows you act on things – that is, *his* things. A lackadaisical approach may be met with a casual attitude in return. I once asked a client for a year's bank statements that she got sent weekly. I was given about 50 unsorted, unopened envelopes in a pile. I was pretty disgusted and the lady in question got the short shrift she deserved.

11

SELF-EMPLOYED

Don't expect your accountant to be aware of all the tax rules. There are millions of them. He will be an expert in some, have a general awareness of most and be ignorant of a few. If you catch him out on something he does not know, *do not* automatically think he is a bad accountant.

SELF-EMPLOYMENT

Essentially you are self-employed if you are a sole trader or in partnership. Property rentals also falls into self-employment but with its own special tax-allowable rules.

Mortgage companies define directors of their own limited companies (bizarrely) as self-employed.

While we go on to lament the advantages of self-employment in terms of getting your tax lower there are some disadvantages. You are not on a regular monthly wage, have no sick pay or maternity leave. You do not get a contributory pension scheme. You lose the job security you might have and you have new responsibilities for VAT and tax. Above all, you are completely on your own (unless in partnership).

EXPENSES

Of great concern to the self-employed are the expenses that can be claimed. Your accountant should know what these are. They are laid down by a broad set of rules in tax law, and by general convention. However, there is a certain amount of judgement or discretion involved when it comes to the allowability of these expenses.

Accountants can differ in the treatment of these costs, basically due to their attitude towards the risk of queries. Accountants without much experience can overreact one way or the other. If you accountant overreacts on the side of caution you could well end up paying more tax than with another accountant who will take a more favourable risk-assessed judgement with expense claims. Experience helps here and the accountant who has had a lot of taxman dealings should have a better grasp of how far he can go for you.

Certain expenses that have a personal use such as motor expenses, as well as general allowances for spouse's assistance and use of home, fall into this category. It is unlikely that your accountant will raise these with you in a meeting as he will just want to apply his or his firm's policy and not have you saying what you want here. It is usually the case that clients are guided by their accountant simply because they have no knowledge of anything different. However, there are many variants of treatment of these kinds of expenses given by different advisors.

I have had comments in the past like 'My accountant thought he was working for the Inland Revenue, not me'. You do want one who is working for you, not for HM taxman, and it may be that he needs a bit of pushing in the direction of getting a bit more for you. You are likely to meet some resistance and arguments such as 'This is what we do for other clients', and you may counter this with 'I will take full responsibility' – but of course you will have to be quite confident. It's all your responsibility anyway, so you are not giving away much except an equivalent retort.

We are not talking about serious issues like things being left out of the accounts. It is just the application of judgement. As long as you have some basis for what you claim, you can have a good argument. If your accountant has asked the right questions to understand your personal situation then you should be getting the best advice on your expenses, especially if he realises you are on the ball about it.

GET THE KNOWLEDGE

The HMRC website has a vast database of knowledge on offer, so why not take advantage of this free resource. Unlike much online information, this website is authoritative and factually reliable. You might think that you do not want to bother with it, but do not be afraid to search on it. You will be amazed at the knowledge it will give you.

For example just look at the list it gives you of things you can claim for as a self-employed person

> *Phone costs, mobile, fax and internet bills, postage, stationery, printing, printer ink and cartridges, computer software your business uses for less than 2 years, computer software if your business makes regular payments to renew the licence (even if you use it for more than 2 years), rent for business premises, business and water rates, utility bills, property insurance, security, using your home as an office (only the part that's used for business),vehicle insurance, repairs and servicing, fuel, parking, hire charges, vehicle licence fees, breakdown cover, train, bus, air and taxi fares, hotel rooms, meals on overnight business trips, uniforms, protective clothing needed for your work, costumes for actors or entertainers.*

Your employee and staff salaries, bonuses, pensions benefits, agency fees, subcontractors, employer's National Insurance, hiring of accountants, solicitors, surveyors and architects for business reasons, professional indemnity insurance premiums, bank, overdraft and credit card charges, interest on bank and business loans, hire purchase interest, leasing payments, alternative finance payments, e.g. Islamic finance, advertising in newspapers or directories, bulk mail advertising (mailshots),free samples ,website costs, event hospitality, trade or professional journals, trade body or professional organisation membership if related to your business

Your accountant will not run through that list with you at the year end, so make sure you do it yourself. Before you send in your books to your accountant see if there is anything from it you can add. It is a useful memory-jogger. Something that may have been paid for outside your normal payments or a gift can still be included.

SELF-EMPLOYED OR NOT?

Here is a fact not every accountant will tell you.

For small businesses there are financial and other benefits to having a self-employed workforce.

This goes against the standard professional coverage, the advice from 'remote' accountants, the large firm's managers or an accountant that does not particularly like you. Many people in small business know it. Accountants won't say it, they are veering into dangerous territory so why should they?

164

We have been in a battleground of self-employment verses employment for many years. The employer and employee will pay less tax in a self-employed arrangement than in an employee one. HMRC will get more tax in an employed one. So we have a battle of needs in a murky area of law.

So if you ask your accountant what the rules are for being self-employed, you might well get a variety of answers. Some accountants have particular tests they champion. Some stick rigidly to how they interpret the law. Some may tell you to take your chances. It's always been a bit nebulous, so in fact you might get vague answers.

Often the self-employed think that if they work for more than one employer they can be classed as self-employed. However, HMRC do not take that into account, it is the *nature* of the relationship that determines the status, not the *number* of relationships.

If we look at the business entity tests that have been published by HMRC we get some clarification and there is a useful points scoring system. I have divided them into three sections that each creates points indicating your self-employed status.

Scoring less than 10 points means you are in trouble. Over 20 you are fine, in between you are in arguing territory. Watch out for the big minus at the end. So let's go through it.

1. The big issues

	Points scored
Assistance test	35
Substitution	20
Business premises test	10
Efficiency test	10

The **assistance** test means you pay someone to work with or for you. This creates the most points. They need to bring in fees so are actually doing some work. Basically if you have this there is never any dispute you are self-employed. A whopping 35 points.

Being able to **substitute** someone else for you is a great scorer but this can be difficult and rare. Even in big firms, clients want a certain person doing the work. Scores 20 points. Good to have in a contract even if not used.

If you actually pay out for **business premises** then you are on a winner. This is not just use of your dining room for which you create a charge to yourself.

The **efficiency** test is about increasing your income. That is it is not just fixed. The same amount going out each month will not look healthy.

Bad debts? Yes businesses have these, not employees, so 10 points if you have – not great compensation.

2. Getting supporting points

<u>**Points scored**</u>

Repair test – put right mistakes?	4
Indemnity Insurance – needed	2
Advertising -spend over £1,200	2
Billing test – do you invoice	2
Business plan – done one	1

To get the repairs points you have to put right mistakes at your own cost. As this is quite fundamental, you get 4 points.

The rest score little, but at least if you have all these you do get over 10.

3 The big negative

Have you been on PAYE with them before?
MINUS 15

If you take on board these points you are likely to know more than your accountant.

SELF-EMPLOYED DIRECTORS

Directors have special circumstances. If you ask your accountant if, as a director (of your own company), you can go self-employed, you are likely to get a quick answer: No! This is because if HMRC found out they would disallow it and your accountant's knuckles could get rapped. You can get away with it only in a few specialised circumstances such as film and TV companies. Where they have a separate budget for a film, then a director of the company doing the production may put in a self-employed '(film) directors fee'.

THE TAX YOU PAY

How many times have you heard: 'I've got a great accountant – I paid hardly any tax last year'? It sounds initially a reasonable point. But it is full of holes. Some people superficially judge their accountant on how much tax they pay. They measure this against a yardstick of what they *think* they should pay but often they have no real idea of what that is. It's either based on a hunch, what they paid before or what their mates pay. Each of these can lead you wildly astray and to false premises and arbitrary conclusions. Everybody's circumstances are different for tax, even if they appear similar on the surface. Tax can often be more than you expected or less, not very often the same as what you expected.

There are a number of distorting measures inherent in the system which can create widely false expectations. Suddenly when you are told the amount of tax to pay your first thought might be, 'Has my accountant got it right'? So, how can you check you are paying the right tax? Basically you can't. Unless you get your affairs re-done there is no sure way to know if the tax you pay is right. You rely on having that good accountant telling you correctly.

HONEST TAX RATES

A reason for appearing more than expected is the separating of National Insurance from the headline rates of income tax in the press. The headline rate may be 20% but then as National Insurance (class 4) is paid with your 20% tax as one payment, suddenly your tax rate is nearer 30%. In the section below, we see the tax plus National Insurance rate can go up to 62% Where have you ever heard that published as the top rate of tax?

National Insurance is just another form of income tax. Governments have been trying to amalgamate the two into one 'tax' for years. The Conservative chancellor *Nigel Lawson* made valiant attempts to do this but found it too difficult. The trouble with such changes is there are winners and losers and if the losers are too big a group of voters then it goes in the political dustbin, however worthwhile it may be. *The Office of Tax Simplification* has as its number one task the merging of tax and National Insurance. This is long overdue, and I suspect it is proving more difficult than they imagined. If it goes through there will be winners and losers and the losers' loss will, no doubt, be championed by the press.

So, if you group together National Insurance and tax and show them as just one rate let's see how the percentages change in the table (2013/14 rates) below. For starters when we take National Insurance payments into account the tax-free amount of £9,440 comes down to £5,725. Again, this is not what the press champion on the back of the politicians' spin.

First	£5,725	0 %
Then to	£7,755	£140
Then to	£9,440	9%
Then to	£41,450	29%
Then to	£100,000	42%
Then to	£118,880	62%
Then to	£150,000	42%
Over	£150,000	47%

NATIONAL INSURANCE

Understand the basic differences in National Insurance. It's not hard and should not be a mystery. There are just four types known as classes:

Class 1 is paid by those on PAYE – they have no choice.

Class 2 is the ridiculous hangover from the 'weekly stamp' that you pay directly as self-employed (currently £2.50/week). It's so pitiful that accountants often failed to mention it completely and if you had not registered you could have gone on for years without paying it and get penalised on your pension for 'forgetting'. Make sure you have not 'forgotten' it in the past. But the system now is automatic when you first register online as self-employed, somewhat correcting the old system for new self-employed registrants.

Class 3 is a voluntary contribution – I have yet to find anyone who pays this.

Class 4 is the surcharge that self-employed people pay on their profits – your accountant tells you this figure when he tells you your tax for the year and you pay them both together. He deals with that one but *not* the Class 2. Most tend to just link this in with their tax payment as they are always paid together.

To check your situation ring or write directly to the NI contributions office and ask them for a summary of your contributions to date: *HMRC, Benton Park View, Newcastle upon Tyne, NE98 1ZZ; telephone 0845 302 1479.*

THE MISLEADING 'PAYMENTS ON ACCOUNT'

Another reason for your tax appearing to be higher than expected is the system of advance payment which applies. Your tax demand will include payments 'on account', meaning payment for the future based on your previous tax return. This skews the system as far as trying to correlate the payments you are making.

When your profits are increasing year by year you get hit with a double whammy. When it comes to 31 January you have to pay the 'catch-up' tax for the increase on the year just gone. At the same time you get asked for increased payments on account based on these increased profits. This can seem high and out of proportion to your earnings. It is not your accountant's fault. It is the application of the tax laws following the infamous 'self-assessment'.

Watch out for some warning signs of higher tax from your accountant. He may not have done your accounts so will not know your tax liability, but if you have been telling him how business has been booming he may slip into conversation *'you need to allow for a large tax bill next January'*. Do not ignore these little words of warning. Get prepared.

MAKING A TAX PROVISION

Self-employed tax is due on 31 January and 31 July. You need to build up a fund over the year to pay these demands when due or you will face paying interest and surcharges. But, as can be seen from the hugely varying rates above, you cannot know in advance exactly what you will have to pay until after April at the earliest.

Your accountant cannot tell you what the tax next January is going to be in advance of doing your tax return, sometime after April or often approaching Christmas. What's more, until those accounts are final, there can be changes or adjustments that make substantial differences to your tax – up or down. Your accountant will be cautious about giving you a tax figure until he has done all the work.

Accountants may advise that an average, 'small', self-employed person should put aside 20% of their income (before expenses) and this should just about cover their tax bill, or at least the main chunk of it. However, this is generalisation and you could need to double this if you fall into a higher tax bracket. All sorts of factors can affect the final tax bill, most of which will depend on your circumstances and not on the work of your accountant. For fairly simple tax accounts the accountant can make small differences to the tax you pay by his approach to expenses – but usually not that much.

So don't expect that tax figure until your accountant has had time to produce your accounts and complete your tax return. It makes sense, then, not to leave things to the last minute, say, to Christmas time or even later. Get everything in well before. He will appreciate that and you will know your tax liability as early as possible.

GETTING A BEST ESTIMATE

Look at last year's profit per the accounts your accountant did. Then estimate the increase that is happening this year. Come to a 'best guess' for your net profit for this coming financial year. Do all this yourself – you are the best judge for this guess. Then email this figure to your accountant and ask him what your tax payments would be based on this profit. If he is competent he can put it into his computer and in a few minutes have all your payments and payments on account for a year in advance. This can be invaluable to you in putting away an amount to cover your tax. **But you must give him the profit figure. He needs to get this from you as he will not want to guess.**

REDUCING PAYMENTS ON ACCOUNT

You can apply to reduce your payments on account to as much as NIL. Accountants are not always happy to do this, especially when it comes from clients who just don't have the money right now. This is because when the next year comes around you can get a huge tax bill (two years' worth) plus interest on the non-payments on account. Some can even get into a syndrome of wanting to postpone every year, looking on it as a loan from HMRC. Your accountant will not favour this; in fact, he may well just refuse to do it for you.

But it is not all bad news. The converse applies when your profits are decreasing and you suddenly get a refund.

REFUNDS

However, refunds occur quite naturally in self-assessment and PAYE where the system requires some form of 'payment on account'. It is not your accountant's fault that you 'overpaid' with the on account payments, as they are fixed by HMRC in the year before.

You pay an estimate so there will always be an adjustment either up or down. This is just added to your next payment so in fact you do not notice it but it is happening every year.

Refunds are good news and can generate a feeling of gratitude towards your accountant. Refunds are not necessarily the special work of your accountant but they can be; and indeed he can do a good or a bad job on them.

Refunds can also occur because of previous mistakes. That could be mistakes by you or your accountant. You may not realise there was a mistake and just be content with a refund.

I have had cases where clients have not told me they have received a refund directly – possibly hoping it was a mistake in their favour so best to keep quiet.

Do not jump to any particular conclusion when you get a refund. Ask your guy for the reason.

LOSSES

Good accountants will get you extra special tax refunds by maximising your relief when losses occur. When you make a loss there is a choice to either carry it forward or set off and get a refund. Make sure your accountant is not opting for the lazy way of carrying it forward and denying you a refund. Remember, if you see the word 'Loss' anywhere on your final financial statements ask yourself – where is this getting relieved?

If you don't know ask your accountant. Make sure you are maximising this loss against tax somewhere. Unrelieved losses are a pain you don't feel.

You need to make sure that your losses are not overlooked so let's consider the three types there are. Then, whenever you have seen that little word 'Loss' you can check you are getting the best treatment.

1. Opening year losses

When you start in business it is not uncommon to make a loss in the first year (or years). The tax system allows you to set losses off against other taxable income (often PAYE) you may have had up to *three years* before you started. Getting a refund is fairly standard stuff. But has your accountant done all he could?

Accountants can go an extra mile or two even here. For creative or proactive accountants a 'tax loss' can be obtained (created), for example, by introducing capital equipment, prior expenses or 'extra' costs in that first year. A misconception is that equipment has to have been bought in that year. This is not true; you may have been using a computer for pleasure before but now suddenly it becomes a major part of your business. Your accountant can introduce it at a market value to increase your tax losses. So think: is there anything you can bring in that you can tell your accountant about? Be creative – your garage at home is actually crammed full of goods to sell and is now your business storage facility. It cost £5,000 two years ago – bring it in.

Hence you are getting your accountant acclimatised to maximising your tax losses by telling him what you use in your business that may be 'off books'. You are making him into a creative one. Your help in this regard and that little extra 'push' is the special ingredient.

This is especially important in these first years, as these losses can not only be set back against the tax you have paid in previous years but can generate an interest supplement from HM taxman. For the first time you can get the taxman to pay *you* interest. If you were previously a higher rate taxpayer, the refunds can be huge. The taxman backdates the interest to when you paid the tax. On top of that, your refund is, of course, tax free. I once got a refund of more than £100,000 from the taxman for a doctor who had left the NHS to set up privately and whose previous accountant had neglected to claim.

This great tax advantage is there for the taking. It is not tax avoidance. But I have come across a number of accountants who completely forgot to claim this for their start-up clients. The sting is that because of some other random factor the client thinks they have a 'brilliant' accountant – when in fact he is negligent.

Remember how we have seen in other chapters how anyone can claim to be 'an accountant' with letters after their name, even though they have had no formal tax training? This loss relief is the technical stuff which you need to have first learnt with training and then of course apply. This is where the properly qualified accountant with ongoing regulatory updating comes into his own.

So remember, whenever you see that word 'Loss' on your accounts, ask yourself the question: where have I got tax relief for these? Or more importantly ask your accountant. Remember too, that relief for losses is not restricted to just the opening years, it can be at any time.

2. Sideways loss relief

When you make a loss during the year to year operating of your trade you can set this off against other income of that year and sometimes of surrounding years. There is a box to tick on your tax return for this. Make sure your accountant has ticked the right one for you.

3. Terminal loss relief

If you make a loss in the closing years of your business there is a relief that you can use to set this against profits you made in the three years previously and get a refund. So good accountants will do this automatically. Make sure yours does if this applies.

BOOKS (OR RECORDS)

For many years there were the rules about what records you should keep for limited companies. Keeping 'proper books of account' now extends to all people in business, which includes the self-employed, of course. You can now be fined for not having proper records. At the very least, you must keep records of all money in and money out with details.

So should your accountant be doing this for you, or telling you what to do for yourself? Some do, some don't, *so ask.*

When I get a new client I always enquire as to how they keep their records. More often than not their system is adequate; most people are conscientious and have this basic requirement in hand. For the few that don't comply I point out what they should keep for their business. Not just for them to be compliant but because I don't want a load of bad records at the year end. You will no doubt want a 'quote' and so your accountant will have to make some assumptions about the records you will keep. If he gives you the quote in writing (like good accountants should) then there should be some qualification that this is based on you keeping good records.

So, ask your accountant's advice and make sure your system is in tune with his from the start. Discuss this at your initial meeting and ask if there are any ways you can make his job easier. Your accountant can design a system of manual recording for you but there is so much standard software out there that you can just adapt. The trouble with accounts software is that it will often offer all the bells and whistles, much of which will be unnecessary for your business. If he recommends particular software to you it may be that his staff are fully au fait with it, and that will make their job easier and hence your costs lower (logically). It is not good to throw at your accountant software he is not used to as you will pay for his learning curve! But even as I am writing this things are moving fast. Cloud-based systems are becoming more and more common, with automatic feeds from your bank to your accountant – pretty impressive. But beware of the warning I issue later on this about having *all your eggs in one basket*.

There is an argument that in a few cases keeping manual books will be more efficient than software, so don't be too rigid. For example a popular book, still available in stationery stores, is the *Simplex* weekly trader. If you keep this it will calculate your VAT and at the year end your accountant just adds up the 52 weeks and produces your accounts incredibly simply. No messing about with getting your software to work, passwords, crashes, getting the appearance of being 'balanced' when no need. A simple method which can be processed by any junior clerk. One important issue is that manual records create a paper trail which your accountant partner can follow to see if the junior member of staff has got it right. This trail gets lost all the time in computers. I am not against computers but you use them when it saves overall time. The trouble is that it's not something clients can easily judge, so do listen to your accountant on this one.

Try not to give unnecessary paperwork to your accountant. Check what he needs; if he sends you a list, stick to that as closely as possible. Extra 'books' may confuse junior staff and cause more time costs on your affairs for 'reading them'.

Make sure your business name is easily visible inside all books and schedules. Accounts clerks might well have several jobs on the go at once and it is possible, though rare, that yours could get mixed up with others. However careful someone is, chaos theory (see later) dictates that one day there will be a mix-up. Your name inside, or visible, on all things is a blessing if this ever happens.

It's easy to think you might just leave something out – who will notice? But clients don't know just how HMRC gets its information and can make some pretty silly mistakes. Fifty-two million people watched *Richard Hatch* take home the first million-dollar prize from the CBS TV show *Survivor*. So what did he do? – he left it off his tax return! In 2006 he got some four years in prison for that and so failing to pay taxes on his $1 million in *Survivor* winnings. A pretty stiff sentence; but then a few years later in 2010 he failed to file further taxes and got another nine months sentence. Some people never learn.

COMPUTER SYSTEMS

There are many computer software systems about for bookkeeping and accounts. All claim they are the best. So how do you pick one? The taxman is not concerned whether you use a computer or not. Neither really is your accountant.

First, do you need one at all? For a small, one-man operation under the VAT limit, probably not. Many years ago I had a plumber who came to me. He was exceptional in that he computerised his affairs. He did not limit it to his bookkeeping, he kept details of all clients, their needs, when the last job was done, how much they paid, how he rated them. All this came out in reports and 'to contact' lists. I told him he should go into IT and forget plumbing. It worked for him because he loved doing it and paid attention to the detail of the input so that it all meant something by being correct. I have had one-man operations under the VAT limit that insisted on keeping their records on *Sage* (a bit of an expensive bookkeeping program for a very small business).

Whatever, your accountant will prefer you to stay away from these until you really need them, just sticking to a simple money in /money out recording system. This can be fine and easy for your accountant (usually his junior staff) to understand. In fact many accountants would prefer that small self-employed persons did not complicate their affairs with elaborate computer systems. Don't assume your accountant will be familiar with your particular computer system and don't think the answer is the most popular accounting system. Some can be excessively complicated for the small business and inadequate input can make it worse for the accountant to unravel.

SPOT CHECKS

HMRC do carry out spot checks on the records kept by the self-employed. This can come in the form of a phone call direct to you out of the blue, asking you what records you keep and how you record 'cash' received. The taxman has twigged that talking to small business clients directly often can indicate transgressions that mean they can go after more tax. They know that an accountant is much more guarded and knows the questions that are coming and hence the answers that should be given. Direct attacks are better for them and one of their first lines of attack is to ask about the records you keep. Make sure you know what you should be recording.

YOUTUBE

There are lots of useful tax tips for the self-employed on *YouTube*. Avoid individuals' diatribes about their own experiences. Look for videos by chartered accountants that prominently display their name. They are most likely to have made a major effort to put it carefully to you and it is most likely to be accurate. Also, do not forget that you can search here too. So, say you are selling a rental property, put that in the search with 'tax' after it.

WHAT ABOUT CASH JOBS?

Accountants will tell you to record all cash received for work done. This is income, is taxable, goes on your tax return and you pay tax on it.

On the other hand, it is not illegal to pay a builder in cash. It is the tradesman who is committing an offence if he fails to declare his full earnings to the taxman. However, if the payer knows that the tradesman will be evading tax (or even has reasonable suspicion of that) then he could be accused of conspiracy to tax fraud. So be careful.

There was a builder called *Harry Rowbottom* who at 58 years old received a knock on the door from the taxman. His response was 'I've been waiting for you for 27 years', He had kept no records of his earnings and always been paid in cash. The taxman guessed he should have paid over £64,000 in tax over the years plus interest. He was jailed in 2012 for 14 months for tax evasion.

COMPANY OR NOT?

One of the things you might do as a self-employed person is consider the move to a limited company. A venture into the unknown, so who better a guide than your accountant you might think. So is he giving you the best advice on this move?

While the limited liability status of operating through a company is the defining difference, many will feel that operating through a company will save them tax. However, this is not always the case.

The maximum rate of company tax (known as corporation tax), has been around 20% but is now decreasing and this contrasts with personal tax rates of 40% to 45%.

The consistent lowering of corporation tax over the years and the introduction of the magical £10,000 tax-free profits by *Gordon Brown* led to a flurry of company formations through from 2002 to 2006.

The smallest traders were told by their accountants to form a limited company to save tax. Because of the £10,000 tax-free band, this was true. After its abolition in 2006, it wasn't. The smaller traders suddenly became worse off. So the small traders with low profits were suddenly paying more tax and accountancy fees.

Some went back to being sole traders, others stayed as companies. Accountants' advice on this varied throughout the country.

There is a basic issue to understand with a company. You pay the company tax on your profits, *then* you have to pay more tax to get the profits out of the company into your personal hands. This is the problem that faces all small company owners.

You accountant has various choices in tackling this issue (explained to some extent in Chapter 12 highlighting how your knowledge in this tricky area will get him working at his peak.)

Forming a company means more work for your accountant and therefore higher fees, so he will look favourably if you indicate a tendency to set one up. He may even persuade you to do it. After all, the upping of fees is of major concern to accountants, so don't presume that your accountant is superhuman and that is not a consideration.

With the formation of your company, your accountant has a vital new role – the balancing of your salary and dividends. Suddenly you are thrust into a new area of tax that you may not have encountered before. Your accountant has become the teacher and you the pupil. Your own control over your affairs is reduced and that may feel uncomfortable.

PROS AND CONS

Generally company formation considerations are:

<u>Pros</u>

Limited liability
Status
Ownership flexibility
Possible *lower* tax

<u>Cons</u>

Audits
Costs
More admin
Sometimes *higher* tax

12

DIRECTORS

You would think you could put this simple question to your accountant and get a simple answer

> Will I save tax by incorporating?

The trouble is that is a loaded question, the true answer being

> It depends.

Depends on what? All these:

> Your turnover/profits
>
> What loans you take
>
> Future tax rates
>
> Budget changes
>
> Company ownership
>
> How much you draw out

These are pretty big variables and there is no one-size-fits-all answer – each of the above factors has to be carefully considered in relation to your particular business situation and estimations on potential tax liabilities made.

This means a quick answer from your esteemed accountant will equally be loaded. He might make judgements on these issues himself and give you a firm answer. He might be swayed by the extra fees and give you that firm 'yes' you were waiting for. He will not want to appear wishy-washy but that will be his true calling on this subject because he knows how those variables could all actually turn against you and you then end up paying more in tax.

COMPANY TAX

When you first move from being a sole trader to a company you enter a new world of taxation. It is unlike what you have experienced before and seems to be something that only your accountant understands. Confusing concepts that seem to defy logic, like dividends, become his domain. The effect of this is that your accountant becomes – or seems to – more powerful.

In a company, the allowances for expenses and rules for income determination are basically the same as for self-employed, but how you pay your tax differs completely. A basic understanding of the system, without getting into detail, is most useful in dealing with your accountant so that when he tells you about the allocation of profits, dividends and drawings, and how it affects the tax you pay, it will not seem like magic. So let's look at the basics.

There are three taxes that apply in a company (unlike just one for the self-employed). These three all contribute to the total tax you pay under this system and the optimum use of each one is key. Your accountant is unlikely to explain it in this easy way. Keeping a bit of mystery will suit him.

- First, the company's **profit** will be taxed. This is corporation tax.
- The second tax that affects you is **PAYE** on your salary or benefits. Your aim here will be to keep your monthly PAYE payments to a minimum. PAYE is wonderful for the government because it brings in millions but

pretty nasty for those who have no choice but to pay it. As a company owner you do not want to 'overpay' PAYE thereby creating a company *loss*. This is because, unlike corporation tax, any PAYE excesses in the year cannot be clawed back next year if profits dive. So that's the second tax to consider.

- The third tax is an extra **personal tax** you will suffer on any other drawings from the company. These can be excess dividends, overdrawn loan accounts or items/services taken for personal use and benefits in kind.

So, with these three taxes to consider, your aim is to make them all as low as possible. Your accountant will love explaining to you how your dealings have impacted on you during a financial year when he has drawn up the accounts. How some of your excesses now have to be paid for, or how your prudence means plenty of cash after tax. He should be dealing with the final adjustments and mitigating your problems either at a meeting or when finalising the accounts. The questions are, has he done all he can? How far is he going for you?

So let's have a bit more background on those factors.

TAKING A SALARY AND DIVIDEND

Many people start their company from scratch, with simple company ownership. The advice most accountants give is to take a small salary and top it up with dividends. There are three valid reasons for this: you get the tax-free salary element, you cover your minimum National Insurance contributions thereby protecting your pension, and you optimise the 20% corporation tax rate with dividend extraction up to the top of the applicable tax band.

It's fairly simple, straightforward advice at this stage and many accountants would be happy to just leave it at that – and many do.

POST 6 APRIL 2016

A big change in the taxation of dividends arrived in April 2016. Before, there were quite generous savings to be made (under the right conditions). If you were a single-person company with profits of about £100,000 you would have a potential saving of £5,000 pre April 2016. Post April 2016 this now drops to £700. Hardly worth the extra accountancy fees.

The system now is that individuals can earn up to £5,000 in dividends without any charge to tax. After this level you will suffer tax at 7.5%, 32.5% or 38.1% depending on your tax band.

So small businesses are going to pay more in tax. The question is:

**Is my accountant going to tell me
to go back to being self-employed
in the light of this change?**

Unlikely, unless you are a **favoured client**.

What has happened now is that your incorporation status is even less tenable and getting you out of it is a pain for your accountant. The last thing your accountant would want is to change you over then find, when circumstances alter, that you would have been better off in the limited company after all.

TAKE A RAIN CHECK

With these changes it's a good time for fresh look at your circumstances. You could undertake this yourself or do it in conjunction with your accountant. The three issues you need to look at are:

1. Am I saving tax?

Consider the position of being self-employed versus operating through a limited company. Estimate your future profits and do calculations for each. See what the savings will actually be. Look at other expenses such as administration, accountancy fees, Companies House.

2. Do I want the benefit of Limited Liability?

This is the overriding reason for having a limited company. Your personal assets are protected (bank guarantees excepted) and I am sure you all know that. With this minimal difference in tax this becomes the major reason for operating the business this way.

3. Do I want other benefits?

There are other benefits such as status, formal sets of rules, shareholders shares, succession issues and a few more. These can well be a consideration. Look at these issues and how they affect *you*.

Set up a meeting with your accountant if you want clarification and a *final* decision.

END OF YEAR BALANCING

When it comes to the end of the year there is a balancing act to perform unless you have had a rigid system, which most small companies do not. Things are simple if your director's loan account is in credit and your dividends and salary keep you under the basic rate of tax. Your accountant's standard advice has been spot-on and you have optimised your tax position.

But many have to take more from their company or use it for personal expenses and find that keeping within the basic rate is just not an option with their personal expenses.

There may also be other shareholders who do not deserve a dividend and/or the company may not have enough reserves to pay a dividend.

This is where the end of year balancing act comes into play and your accountant should start to earn his money as this accounts finalisation becomes even more important. The variables can be daunting, even to an accountant. This form of finalisation is not taught in exams – it is learnt through experience.

THE DIRECTOR'S LOAN ACCOUNT

We now look at a very important topic that affects all small company owners: the director's loan account. It can be called other names – director's current account, loan account, drawings account, director's capital account – but its most popular name, and as used by HMRC, is the director's loan account. If it mystifies you, read this section again. If you want to get the best tax position, then prompting your accountant on this topic pays dividends.

The operation of the director's loan account is a vital part of the annual finalisation of accounts. The partner or senior accountant will examine this as part of the final reviews of the accounts. The first factor they consider is whether its balance is in debit or credit. Debit means the director owes the company money and credit means the company owes the director money.

Consider you have just opened an ordinary bank account with the XYZ bank. You open it with £5,000 of your own money, draw some out and incur some charges, and get some interest. Your statement would look something like the following:

```
XYZ BANK – BANK STATEMENT

Mr A G Client

                        DEBIT    CREDIT

Money paid in                    5,000

Bank Charges            100

Money withdrawn        2,000

Interest credited                 500

                       ----------  ----------

                Balance  £3,400
```

(in credit or money in the bank)

We would all agree that you have a credit balance with the bank of £3,400.

Now, instead of a bank, substitute your company and consider similar value transactions with your company.

```
XYZ COMPANY – DIRECTOR'S LOAN ACCOUNT

Mr A G Client

                               DEBIT    CREDIT

Money lent to company                   5,000

Nanny paid by company          100

School fees paid by company    2,000

Business travel paid personally          500

                              ----------  ----------

                     Balance  £3,400
```

You will see I have mirrored the transactions with things that could occur in your company.

So if you take money out, in whatever form, you get a debit, and if you put money or value back in you get a credit. The secret is getting as many credits as you can.

The director's loan account operates in just the same way with the company as with your bank account. You can end up in credit or in debit (overdrawn). You will end up overdrawn if you use the company to pay lots of your personal expenses and pay less back, thereby taking drawings.

A word of warning. Do not try and work out what is a *debit* and what is a *credit*, especially by looking at bank statements; you will end up in knots. Also do not use those words with your accountant; it will confuse him. Just use 'Money in' and 'Money out'.

There are two main items that pay back drawings on your account and take it back towards credit: dividends and salary. The most common situation – and standard advice from your accountant – is to vote a basic salary each month throughout the year, operating PAYE and NI on this and paying it over; then at the end of the year voting a dividend to cover the excess drawings taken and bring your director's loan account back into credit by the end of your financial year.

Unfortunately, it's not always that simple. Companies that have no reserves (basically an insolvent balance sheet) are prohibited from dividends by company law. If you do vote for dividends then HMRC can ignore it and tax you more. Know if your company has no reserves. Ask your accountant or look at the balance sheet. These come about from usually one of two things, or both. Years of bad trading or taking too much money out.

Accountants hate director's loan accounts to be in *debit* (director owes money to company) at the end of the year as this causes problems. HMRC requires a debit disclosure on a separate form and at the same time requires you to pay tax on the debit balance.

To avoid a debit, accountants will usually suggest an extra bonus or dividends, leaving their client to pay the extra tax. They will easily justify this with 'They have had the money, they must pay the tax'.

But you really gain if you can employ some creative thinking to get you past this hurdle and not just immediately succumb to this extra tax. This is your accountant going the extra mile for you. If he starts suggesting extra things that can be put in to get you back towards credit, give him 10 points.

Some ideas for credits to your director's loan account you might like to suggest to your accountant:

- Parking meters fed during the year

- Subsistence costs borne personally

- Use of home as office, contribution to light and heat

- Home telephone costs

- Own equipment used in business

- Overseas travel to see potential customers

- Home internet costs

- Sky subscription (if you are in the media business or have a work need)

- Redecoration of home office

- Computers bought personally and used for business

- Mileage allowance if you use your own car

- Chauffeurs or taxis

- Wages for spouse for telephone answering

- Home studios

- Building of garage/shed for storage of files or materials

- Entertaining paid personally

- One last, extreme case – building an annexe at home for use as office

THE EFFECTIVE USE OF THE LOAN ACCOUNT

To minimise your tax you want the best form of effective use of this director's loan account. Your third party accountant will not automatically go this extra mile for you; you need to be that **favoured client**. But you may as well understand what can be done and even if your accountant has not gone there for you these are still your accounts. As long as your arguments are reasonable, your accountant will have to put them through when prompted.

So let's consider how this could work in your favour…

You run a small company making profits each year. The company is set up with you and your wife or partner owning 50% each, but you do the main work. Although your partner does a few things, such as organising lunches, she does not really look at it as 'work'.

Consider your company has made a profit of £100,000 (pre April 2016) before you took any monies. If you were on

PAYE you would pay nearly £35,000 in taxes, leaving you £65,000 in your hand.

Using your director's loan account as follows, the tax drops to £15,000, saving you a whopping £20,000 in tax. Let's see how this works:

XYZ COMPANY – DIRECTOR'S LOAN ACCOUNT		
Mr A G Client		
	DEBIT	CREDIT
Nanny paid by company	100	
Drawings	85,500	
Director's salary		9,500
Wife's wages		8,500
Mileage allowance		4,000
Use of home -utilities		1,050
Dividend voted at year end		30,000
Dividend for wife		30,000
Business travel paid personally		600
Computer bought personally		2,000
	-----------	----------
	Balance £50 (in credit)	

The voted dividends are just below the higher rates, meaning no extra tax. You and your wife will pay a small amount of National Insurance on the wages but that will keep your pension entitlement in place. The only tax is the corporation tax at 20% on the profits of £100,000, reduced by relief for wages and other charges to £15,000.

So in the end you are £15,000 better off with the money in your hand. Some accountants are not always forthcoming about the power of the director's loan account – but, now you know about it, so they had better beware.

The changes post 5 April 2016 would mean you have an extra liability of two times £25,000 dividend at 7.5% (the first £5,000 is free of tax) making an extra liability of £3,750 but you are still £11,250 better off. Also corporation tax rates are dropping.

Ask your accountant for a copy of your director's loan account each year. Look at the entries. Any you do not understand – ask about.

DIVIDING DIVIDEND INCOME

Most accountants will advise that, to save tax, the company's shares are split between married couples, thus taking advantage of personal allowances and resulting in lower rates for both partners. When your accountant sets up your company he should advise on the share allocation, especially if you are being charged a premium by your accountant for company formation over what it would cost you to do it yourself on the net. It now only costs £15 to form a company – any charges over this should relate to your accountant's input. This can validly be anywhere between £100 and £1,000.

Make sure you consider with him what the optimum shareholding is for your family situation to pay the least tax.

DIVIDEND DOCUMENTATION

What documentation should small companies keep when paying dividends? Accountant's views differ on this subject. You may take the cautious approach whereby he will insist that you document minutes of meetings declaring the dividends and do dividend vouchers. Of course processing more paperwork entails extra charges to you the client, so is it really necessary?

Some go as far as insisting that you have a meeting with yourself and document your decisions. This is clearly lunacy. The Companies Act 2006 did go some way to modernising company law in this digital age but sadly not as far as they could – so some antiquated habits remain.

Irrespective of the law, your accountant may claim that all this documentation is needed in case you have an HMRC investigation and in case they disallow the dividend. There is an element of truth in this but there are in practice only two situations where a valid (that is wanted by all) dividend can be disallowed by HMRC:

1. When the company has insufficient reserves (net assets for short) to declare the said dividend
2. Where HMRC consider there is tax avoidance going on and they want to be seen to be taking action

Legislation also considers in its reasoning the date point as relevant to outside shareholders but this is irrelevant to the proprietary-owned company.

If you have an accountant who appears to be overzealous in his commitment to pointless paperwork then there is a solution. After you receive the first salvo of seemingly irrelevant documentation do not try to reason the practical approach. Simply thank your accountant for doing this but tell him you will prepare your own paperwork on dividends from now on. Copy what he has done, just advancing the date and any quantum of dividend as you go. If you have shareholders who have their own tax returns to do then giving them dividend vouchers is a good measure. Producing your own vouchers is simpler than using a train ticket machine and takes less time too. Do them yourself.

But remember the system was changed on 6 April 2016, so don't copy the ones previous to that. Now there is *no* tax credit. Some will say you do not need dividend vouchers anymore, some will say you do.

LEAVING MONEY IN THE COMPANY

You will save greatly on tax if you can leave profits in the company. This means you have enough to live on, so don't need to draw all the profits and can just pay the corporation tax rate of 20% instead of the 45% higher rate tax.

The trouble is, most owners are not in the position to leave profits in the company and gain this super tax advantage. You can effectively leave money in the company by buying assets or pension contribution. There are tax advantages to be had but this all involves you having some surplus funds. Basically, you are a successful, wealthy businessman if you can do this, demonstrating that effective use of a company in this way can be a real tax-saving device. But most of our assumptions so far are based on the need to draw all the profits out.

The sting is that usually when you are in this wealthy position you would have a company for the other reasons, such as the limited liability protection. Hence this tax advantage can be a red herring.

CARS

Most people will use a car of some sort in their business and one of the common questions to ask your accountant is:

'How should I account for/buy the car to get the maximum tax saving?'

The real answer the accountant should give is, 'I don't know' – that is unless he can predict how many miles you are going to do over the next year and what the car expenses will be.

There are two ways you can deal with a business car: one is the mileage rate and the other the actual costs. Mileage rates are currently 45p first 10,000 and 25p thereafter. Let's say you do 12,000 business miles, then that is a claim of £5,000 (tax free) that can be made. Compare this with a capital allowance of £1,700 plus petrol of £2,000, insurance and servicing of £1,300 and you arrive at the same total. Your accountant will probably plump for just one, so as not to appear to be a ditherer.

Of course, if it's a company car (which you did not pay for out of personal expenses?) you get a tax charge on top. But as you did not pay for it personally you cannot claim the mileage allowance anyway.

EMPLOYING SPOUSES AND CHILDREN

The rules here are that, to be allowable for corporation tax, they must be paid a 'market rate' for an 'actual' job. Who defines those two things is another matter. This is a grey area that accountants will try to avoid, as they don't want any comeback. If you are going to do this, make sure you emphasise the actual job done so he does not have any misgivings that it is valid.

He should then put it through as allowable for corporation tax. But don't expect an easy ride on this one. You may have to convince him that your kids really do do valuable work that justifies the pay.

THE MINIMUM WAGE

To avoid this applying to you as a director, simply do not have a contract of employment. It is generally accepted that the national minimum wage regulations do not apply in this situation.

DIRECTOR'S EXPENSES

A director may incur expenses on the company's behalf – travel and accommodation, say – and then get them reimbursed from the company. The company will claim corporation tax relief on this payment but that's not the end of the story. There is an obligation on the company to complete a P11D form for these expenses and on the director to enter them on his personal tax return. It is a paper-chasing exercise and the director then has to submit a claim that these expenses are wholly, exclusively and necessarily incurred for the purposes of the employment. I have not known many directors who say they are not.

ACCOUNTANTS' VIEWS

I called up a few accountants claiming to be a new client with a small company in the video business. After I managed to get some prices for the work (with some difficulty), I came to my final question:

> **I have taken a salary of £20,000 and dividends of £20,000 in the year and have found I have an overdrawn (debit) balance on my director's loan account at the end of the year of £30,000. What would be your advice?**

The difference in answers was staggering. To generalise it went like this:

Unregulated firms – generally thrown by the question to the point of stuttering.

Small regulated firms – launched into a logical dissemination of tax law without giving any advice.

Larger firms – would not give anything for free; said they would have to have a lot more details and that I'd have to become a client.

So to judge from this very unscientific survey there were one or two small regulated firms who were on the ball. You need to make sure your own guy is.

13

INVESTIGATIONS

I had a client who had served three years in prison for an assault when he was a teenager. He was full of remorse and turned into one of the most helpful people to all he met. He told me one thing about his time inside I remembered:

'You cannot fight the system and win'.

HMRC have one of the biggest systems going. You have to learn how to play the game. Firstly, understand some basic rules, then get your accountant to play your hand.

THE FIRST LETTER

The system of self-assessment basically means you send in your details with the calculation of your tax due (or rather your accountant does) and then pay it. That's it – year by year. Many go on like this throughout their lives quite happily.

HMRC's power comes with their ability to 'investigate' any details sent. They have their ways of deciding who to investigate. These are not publicised but can follow on from things such as abnormalities in the return, tip-offs, press or internet information, status, history and, somewhat rarely, the advisor you use. There is an overall limit of about a year from the filing deadline to start questions. However, in cases of negligence or fraud there is no time limit.

So that 31 January following the previous deadline is an important milestone. If a letter comes (maybe mid-January) asking some initial questions then take things seriously. Get engaged with your accountant and start sorting it out. Never ignore it or your accountant's requests.

GUILTY FIRST

In tax law you are *guilty* first. You must then be able to prove to the taxman your *innocence*. So you are now going to have to prove that what you sent in was correct, truthful and complied with the law. This extends to estimates you made or valuations.

Say you gave a property to your children. That invokes what is called a capital gain disposal. You need to estimate the value at that gift date. There could be tax due. It is natural to want the value low so you pay the least tax. So you get your friendly estate agent to write to you with a low value. HMRC have a vast data base of valuations – better than your local agent. I have had them arguing with me when I have had three independent estate agents' valuations. You are on the defensive, so get your facts clear to back up those tax returns.

Many will cry 'It's not fair', but it is. It's fair on the majority that pay their fair share of tax because if it were not this way too many people would get out of paying their tax. The onus of proof is a very important concept.

Of course, this is exploited by HM taxman in his duty to collect the most tax, and where better to have a go than at the easy pickings – namely the millions of small 'honest' traders who fall foul in some technical way. The taxman loses his credibility by the way he deals with small traders. This only rationalises the culture of it being fair game to win over the taxman and boast about it in the pub.

THE 'NOTHING WRONG' SYNDROME

I have come across many clients who maintain a fearless attitude of 'I've done nothing wrong'. While a positive confident approach is to be generally applauded, the big downside is that it is not difficult to fall foul of the rules without even knowing it.

The trouble is it's easy to be ignorant of all the myriad rules, so you get caught out on technicalities. HMRC can exaggerate little misdemeanours and then, by their own curious logic, deduce evasion of tax. Suddenly you are a tax evader. Then, with interest and penalties, the 'I've done nothing wrong' guy suddenly owes a lot of money.

FLEECED

I had a client who ran a small pet shop. She had no staff, did it all herself and was not far off retirement age. One special fact was she was actually registered blind. I was amazed at how she moved around her shop and cared for her pets; she had cats, rabbits, birds in cages and bags of pet food. It was her world, she knew it and her animals, and she lived above the shop she rented.

She was previously investigated by HM taxman. The inspector had gone through her bank statements, made wrong assumptions about takings, thereby increasing them, and then assumed the previous years were wrong as well and increased those, too. She had paid some takings into her personal account to avoid bank charges, but these were all noted in a book as best she could. She made hardly any profit and was generally below the taxable threshold. But HMRC exploited her weaknesses in her systems and wrongly claimed she had defrauded on her tax.

She had just £10,000 in savings that she had put aside to buy a caravan for holidays. The taxman took it all by making her sign a contract settlement.

I went back over the year they investigated and I complained to HMRC, pointing out clear errors in their assumptions but they ignored my protestations. I wrote a number of letters but they stonewalled my protests. She had signed the contract and that was it.

Eventually I gave up. Her life had moved on, the pet shop gone and she had got married. My firm had done her accounts for years without charge out of sympathy for what she had been through.

DROPPED IN IT

You need a good accountant to fight your corner. He needs to be experienced to guide you with the right decisions. For example should you put your hands up or stand your ground and fight?

You will need to be honest with him to enable the right decisions to be made. Things have a habit of coming out later. HMRC love to keep rabbits up their sleeves, pulling them out of the hat at opportune times.

I was once in a meeting with an inspector investigating a self-employed builder. The inspector asked him 'Did you do any cash jobs in this year?' Before I could interject the client replied emphatically 'No, none at all.'

I then asked the inspector if I could have a word with my client in private. We went out into the corridor and I said to him (bearing in mind he was a builder) words to the effect of come off it he must know something – you have to own up to an amount for cash jobs. The client was adamant. He claimed that all that year he had been on one major job and, while in other years he had had some cash, in that year he had not had any whatsoever. I said rather unhappily, 'If that's the line you want to play we go back in, but I don't like it.'

We stated 'none' again to the inspector. HM taxman then pushed across the table the copy of an invoice for roof replacement *on my client's notepaper* which said 'Paid £5,000 cash'. My client suddenly went rather quiet. I said 'we have to accept this as an addition', which we did with the inevitable consequences.

When we got outside afterwards I said to him 'you should have told me the truth.' Surprisingly he still was adamant he did. 'But the invoice – that was your notepaper?' He then sheepishly said that a friend had asked him for some blank headed notepaper as he was making an insurance claim. Sometimes even a good accountant can't wave away the problems.

FIVE TYPES OF INSPECTORS

The officious

In comes the guy you are expecting. The archetypal charismatically-challenged inspector of HM Revenue & Customs. He is going to make up for it with his position of investigator. He has seen the police interview in the movies. It's his turn to play now. You know where you stand from the first minute. You are on guard, you are remembering all those things your accountant said to do beforehand. Your answers are so brief they invoke a deadly silence. You want to get out of the meeting as soon as possible.

The guy from the pub

This HMRC guy comes over as 'one of us'. He likes his beer, he says. 'My accountant's warnings were a little bit OTT,' you think. 'This taxman really understands how businesses work and how we have to grease palms occasionally with a bit of cash. I can talk to this guy.' So talk you do. You nail yourself to the wall. HM taxman doesn't need to ask much – everything, all the dodges, it just flows out like coins from a winning one-armed bandit. The HMRC guy, or would-be actor, is a genius who won't be around for long as he will be promoted.

Once my client started empathising with the tax inspector, relaxing and getting on like a house on fire. They talked about each other's holidays and driving in France. When going through the books there was the purchase of a caravan, with a note later saying 'for site'. The client did in fact take it on site for use as an office (rarely) but, as he had told the inspector about his caravan holiday in France, it got thrown out – with all the consequences of submitting wrong accounts.

Mr Dogged

You will come across certain Revenue inspectors that hammer home points like a dog with a bone, extracting everything they can. I had a case where HMRC pursued a person with no house, no family, no car, no significant assets, in fact just debts, for two years after picking up on his hobby on the internet. He did not claim benefit but got by on gifts from his parents, not having to pay rent and some money from his hobby. They kept gunning for him despite me submitting statements of assets showing nothing. Telling them that, even if they got a settlement, they would get nothing. His hobby did exhibit attributes of 'trading' but there was one major missing factor: he did not make any net profit. And he would have done his hobby paid or unpaid. There were long letters, reviews by senior HMRC staff, and more long letters. Cases cited about trading. Arguments back and forth. Eventually I said we would go to a tribunal to sort it out (known as the first tier). Then HMRC gave in and agreed there were no profits up to date covering the last six years. We agreed to do a current tax return and after drawing up the accounts there was no profit. It was a huge waste of Revenue resources. A decision should have been made earlier on.

Mr Fed-Up

Then there is the person who is really fed up with their job. They will skip points quite quickly hoping to land on something that fires them up. Real fraud, for example, not just a bit of extra entertaining claimed.

It has been reported that there are 700 HMRC people looking at high net worth tax savers (I use the phrase tax savers to mean any form of avoidance, evasion or black economy). This is contrasted with 4,700 who go after benefit cheats,

They are fed up that they are not in a more exciting branch of HMRC – maybe.

Detective Columbo

For those not familiar with *Columbo* it was a US TV detective series where the lead character portrayed himself as somewhat dim. This guy asks silly questions as if he was an idiot, but all the time playing with you, taking it all in. Then when you are off guard throwing in the killer question. A descendant of the 'guy from the pub' – watch out for him or her.

SOME RULES TO FOLLOW

Brevity

Your accountant should emphasise the need to answer questions without elaboration. This is most important. Go along with your accountant's advice to the letter on this point and remember the golden rule to only answer the question and *no more*.

Make them wait

If you happen to get the proverbial knock at the door, the general rule is that your accountant deals with the taxman and keeps him from you and it is his job principally to deal directly with them.

If a taxman turns up unexpectedly at your premises asking to see so-and-so or asking a question, ask him to wait in a reception area or the porch. Then go in and phone your accountant. He should tell you exactly what to say *before* you say anything or deal with any questions or queries.

Your 'good' accountant may say 'Go and ask him exactly who he is and which department, ask to see his ID, photocopy it and then come back to me – I will stay on the phone.'

It may turn out to be just the collector of taxes after you because you did not pay the last two months' PAYE. If so, it's fairly straightforward – but the issue could be a more demanding one, and using your accountant in this situation is using him in the best way. He can be your buffer and delay, so use him here.

Helplines

The government has set up various helplines for the general public to speak to them.

There is the general help available for VAT queries and tax. If you go to the HMRC web site you can get all the numbers for these. This advice is free but like anything free there is some caution required regarding the answers.

I know of one case where tax advice given by government departments indicated no tax liability, but later HMRC said there was one. It was about a termination payment to a summarily dismissed employee. The business was told that, if they put in a letter that it was *ex gratia*, then it would be tax-free. Their letter said that but also asked for a confidentiality agreement. HMRC ruled that therefore it was not really *ex gratia* and so not tax free.

Feel happy if you get a satisfactory answer but do be prepared to give your details as they will ask for them so that your query gets onto the database and eventually your file. So don't ask about tax avoidance.

One line is the 'shop them' line where you can tip off HM taxman about what your neighbour or ex-partner is up to. They will want names and addresses and as much detail as you can give them. These tip-offs can save the taxman a lot of investigative work, so they will be very pleasant to you while extracting all they can.

There is also a helpline for tax evaders to call designed to ease them back onto the straight and narrow. The helpline was named *Tax and Benefits Confidential*. The trouble is, it's far from confidential. You will be asked for your name and address, and once you have given these you are done for. If you go on to outline tax evaded then you are jumping into the jaws of a shark, despite what assurances are claimed. So talk to your accountant first; if you want to be eased into the system he is best placed to do it for you.

My advice is, be wary about any direct contact with HMRC. It very easy to fall back on the fact that you really do not have anything to hide, the 'I've done nothing wrong' syndrome, and therefore you can just be *honest*. That's fine in theory but it doesn't always work in practice. Others think, after realising that the taxman is actually human, that he must understand the real world, so it's OK to brag a little. Oh no, every taxman is trained to believe that everyone's a cheat. Their only objective is to catch those cheats (that's everybody) and take them for as much as possible. If they happen to get more than what would have been due, all the better – it's extra brownie points.

Routine visits

Routine VAT visits you can deal with and often it is not cost-effective for your accountant to be with you throughout the visit. But beware of being drawn into questions.

If you feel they are going into dangerous territory, you can still say 'I will have to check with my accountant (*who, of course, has the sort of details I can't provide*) and get back to you'. So you want to try and distinguish between simple explanations and loaded questions. A simple question might be 'Have you got an invoice for this payment?' A loaded question might be 'Have you made any error corrections on past VAT returns?'

The more pleasant, friendly, men/women of the world the inspectors are, the more dangerous they are. A few, simple, light-hearted rules for VAT visits are worth remembering. Some may seem anti-social but you don't want to engage in any socialising. Rules of the game:

- Never get friendly

- Do not offer coffee or tea – let them go out to a shop

- Do not give access to photocopier or phone

- Keep staff away from them – have one person as a contact point

- Turn up the heating so they get sleepy

- At the start say you are available for half an hour now, then again at the end of the visit for any questions

- There will be queries as they go but try and be in another room (or building) where they have to come and knock to ask you something

- If you have claimed back VAT on an annexe and cloakroom, make sure they use that part of the building. How can they then say it's not for business use?

PAYE visits or audits can be worse than VAT visits. The inspectors will be on the lookout for cash payments to cleaners, gardeners, sub-contractors. They will be looking for sub-contractors that they can make a case for being employees. They look for some common mistakes, like missing out National Insurance on cars. Some of the same guidelines above for VAT can be used.

A simple thing like paying your cleaner £20 a week in cash can escalate into a full-blown investigation going back years. The discovery of such a petty cash voucher by an overkeen HMRC checker generates a feeling of well-being because he will feel his day's work is justified.

PAYE settlements for errors are generally more serious matters than individual VAT mistakes often routinely thrown up in a visit. The amounts involved can be much greater, as they can just go back year on year. They are regarded more as 'evasion' matters rather than 'mistakes' for VAT. If you do feel that you have some issues, then your accountant in attendance at these PAYE audits could be a worthwhile investment. Or just ask your accountant to look at your systems with a view to what a PAYE audit might throw up. He should be pretty good at spotting any danger areas.

Pre-meeting briefing

Your accountant should tell you:

- Keep answers short and simple – no elaborating
- Be courteous at all times

211

- Do not 'guess' any answers. Say you don't know or will come back to them
- Refer to me if you are at all unsure about any answer
- If you are ill or cannot make it can it be rescheduled
- Never sign notes. We will make our own

Surprises

Avoid surprises at the meeting. You can do this by your accountant checking with HMRC in advance on a few points:

- Will you be providing an agenda?
- How long shall we allow for the meeting?
- How many HMRC attendees are there?

Venues

There are three choices here. And they are best in this order.

- The agent's (accountant's) premises
- The inspector's
- The client's

INVESTIGATION FEES

Accountants are always upset when their client is singled out for investigation. Their first question will be 'Have we, as a firm, done something wrong?' After they have checked that they have done the accounts right, submitted tax returns based on information they have been told, they breathe a sigh of relief. Then they should devote their attention to helping their client reach a tax settlement with the least amount of pain.

Unfortunately, the first issue will be the question of their fees for dealing with the investigation. If you have taken out insurance, then your fees might be covered. But watch for the small print – for example that you must have 'dealt with your affairs honestly'. This can catch a lot of people out, but then that's insurance for you.

Generally, about 1%, up to a maximum of 5% of accountancy clients are singled out for tax investigations, although you will never know what that percentage is for your accountant. Consequently, junior staff won't have much experience in this field. Accountants have a certain reverence for HM taxman and this could work against you in getting a settlement. They do not want to upset them in case it rebounds on all their clients. Do take an interest in what your accountant is agreeing on your behalf. You can ask your accountant to copy you in on all correspondence with the tax office (he may not like it but he has to comply – 'good' accountants will say, 'Of course'). That way you can see exactly what is being agreed or argued.

So check that your accountant is experienced in investigations as that will count in your favour.

NO TIME LIMIT

Developers *Mr and Mrs Small* got away with their tax deception for 17 years before they were caught. They had three teenage children and both parents were jailed for two to three years for a £4 million tax fraud. The *Smalls* were successful builders and developers in the Northern Ireland property boom that led up to 2008. But, instead of paying the tax on their enormous profits, they salted it away in the Isle of Man asserting they only earned £27,000, and claimed tax credits. It was found that the interest alone on their hidden bank accounts was some £90,000.

They had so much money in the bank that the bank manager travelled over from the Isle of Man personally to see them at home in Ireland. Curiously, they secretly made a video-recording of his visit – which was found when their house was raided by HMRC. The video was totally incriminating, with the banker suggesting ways to hide money and the *Smalls* going along and more. The *Smalls* had to plead guilty after such damning evidence. They had submitted false accounts, false tax returns, false VAT returns. They kept bank accounts and dealings hidden from their accountant. The tax investigators went to customers and used legal powers to force them to get cheques from their bank so they could see that they were paid to the *Smalls*.

The real lesson from the *Smalls* is not what they did. They did what many can do – just don't declare all and hide it. Their amounts were just very large. The amazing fact was that they got away with it for 17 years before being detected. You can never be safe for ever. There is no time limit for HMRC on fraud. Once you have evaded tax, that stays with you for life.

14

FAVOURITISM

Throughout this book we have talked about becoming that **favoured client** and the advantages that brings. If only you had an accountant who really knew his stuff and would apply it to you like he would to his own affairs or those of his family ... But actually it's not impossible to get to that or at least very near to it with the right attitude.

But why do we want to be a **favoured client** ? Using someone's services on a regular basis is no guarantee of quality. The service can be done thoroughly, with care, sloppily, dangerously, fraudulently, aggressively, pro-bono, compassionately. Are you going to send your food back in a restaurant with the risk that the chef then spits in it? Maybe, but treating the staff with a bit of consideration might be more advantageous.

So, if you are on favoured ground how might this be a benefit? I once had a client who ran a profitable high street business as father and son. They had used the same firm of accountants for years. A good respectable firm of chartered accountants who did the same job year after year preparing partnership accounts, agreeing the tax, keeping them informed. They charged a fair and reasonable fee. They did not overcharge but as they did the job the same way year to year, with little partner time, it was a good profitable client for the firm. But there were no extras offered, a classic case of **standard professional coverage**.

The client knew for years that his accountants were a 'bit wet', as he described them, but they were very pleasant and he was reluctant to change for the usual reasons. I was introduced to him and I could see immediately there was scope for a few adjustments to save tax. The client was extremely tax averse, not to the point of fraud or wanting cash. It was just he had this huge bill each year which he felt was too high. Actually it was not; he was taxed on the profits that he made but he was not being shown the best ways to maximise tax savings and it meant he was working (very hard) half the year for the taxman.

It took him some four years after I met him and made some proposals for him to make the change to our firm. He was averse to change, having started his firm from nothing 40 years before and had done things the same way for those many years. When he eventually took the plunge and moved to us he came over with such enthusiasm and praise it was most refreshing. He wanted me at any financial meeting with banks, financial advisors, and he was forward in saying 'make sure you charge me for this', 'you are my accountant for life', 'those others cost me thousands'. So different from clients who criticise your professional advice or moan at charges when they have sent you email after email over the year expecting your time for nothing.

So I was determined to save him as much tax as possible. But how could this be done? His previous accountants had 'done it right'. What more could you do? It seemed impossible.

I mulled over his accounts going through the expenses, seeing if anything might have been left out. Did he do any work at home? 'No' was the answer to that. The capital account on his balance sheet was high and this grabbed my attention. (This is money that is financing the business. It is the build-up of money you have paid tax on but retained in the business for assets or working capital.) Why so high? What can we do about it, that's his money he can't access. This was approaching half a million for him, a very large sum. I could see there were actually two parts to his business – the shop and outside trading. It was at that moment that I saw what could be done.

I set up a company alongside to take over the outside trading part. I then transferred his assets over, giving him a massive credit on his director's loan account (see Chapter 12 for the use of this). This can be done without any tax consequences by moving them at written-down value so it is tax neutral. There are no capital gains as a profit has not been made and they are wasting assets.

Profits then went into the company. The tax rate was now 20% at corporation tax rates meaning 80% of profits were retained in the company. The usual problem is extracting these profits as that extraction incurs further personal tax. However, in this case, because I had moved over his capital account 'assets', he then had thousands as a director's loan to the company. He was then able to draw this out tax free. So suddenly the net effect was he could take his profits out without paying the tax. I had effectively got him out of higher rates and halved his tax bill. This would see him all the way through to his retirement. Bingo!

Everybody's affairs are different but you can see just how advantageous being a **favoured client** is. When you get an accountant 'watching your back' or 'going the extra mile for you', you will reap the rewards. In my above client's case it was hundreds of thousands in tax over the years. All legally done but just applying that extra attention and focused thought for the right result. No complacent accounting. Top advice tailored to the client

So let's look at the ways you can move towards achieving that status with your guy.

BASIC HABITS

There are some basic habits you must adopt. If you fail on a few of these then you are not going to make it at all. Follow these seven habits to move you up from being a standard client to the first level of being that **favoured client.**

1. Don't be an idiot
2. Be honest
3. Be a payer
4. Build rapport
5. Speak to the right person
6. Have an agenda
7. Show your appreciation

Habit 1: Don't be an idiot

We all need a bit of stretching and your accountant is no different. If you basically haven't got a clue about anything, your accountant will fall back on giving you basic explanations.

This will inevitably lead him to keep things simple. He will not be stretching himself to find the better solution for you.

So come armed with some knowledge. If you take on the points I make in this book, you certainly should be in that position.

If you have some specific issues then look them up on *Google* before your appointment. For example:

> You are selling a second property you own and you hear there could be a tax charge. You do not know much about this as you have never come across it before.

A Google search will tell you:

(a) That you can elect that property as your residence and avoid tax.
(b) That the rate of tax is on your gain (i.e. the profit you make), not the sale price.
(c) That the current rate of tax on the gain is 18%
(d) That the first £11,000 or so is exempt from tax altogether.

Suddenly you know much more about your situation. Your accountant does not have to explain these basics and can leap forward to the real tax savings you may be able to use.

Get him focused with your questions. It is your job to keep his eye on the ball. Get your accountant solution-orientated by bringing the talk back if it deviates. Accountants will tend to set out the alternatives and point you towards making the answer. This can be frustrating and confusing. Prompt him and ask questions like 'what would *you* do if this was your property'. The 'if it were you' will really help focus him on solutions and answers he may be intuitively avoiding. If I'm with other professionals and they are saying, 'on the one hand this and on the other hand that' I interject with 'what would *you* do?' and it's amazing how suddenly they get focused on giving an answer.

You can also have a list of questions. This will show him you expect answers. Accountants can respond quite well to written questions as it takes them back to their exam days when life seemed so simple.

However, above all come armed with a bit of knowledge about your personal or business situation.

Habit 2: Be honest

Accountants don't take well to clients who appear dishonest or evasive. If contradictory, misleading statements or even hesitating answers are given then you are likely to going to create a situation which will lead to a guarded approach from your accountant.

For example (and this is taken from an actual case I had) your accountant is going through the books and he comes across a substantial invoice for replacement windows put through as 'office expenses' and the full VAT claimed. The accountant calls the client and queries the invoice; the response is that it was 'for replacement windows at the office'. The accountant looks at the invoice and sees that it actually relates to the client's home, not his office. He knows exactly what is happening; his suspicions are confirmed that the client fraudulently claims expenses whenever possible and furthermore gives false answers. We just put those costs to the director's loan account as drawings; the client never knew that, but it was the correct thing to do.

So you need to be pretty honest with your accountant to get the best service from him. Any display of dishonesty will put him on the defensive and that extra good advice will unlikely be forthcoming. He will default to **standard professional coverage plus extra caution**. Basically, you will worry him that his advice might get tainted somehow by your dishonesty. There are criminal penalties for accountants in this area, much more so than for the ordinary trader. He will distance himself from you as far as possible without letting on.

Remember also the basic fact that if you tell your accountant something he must act on it.

There is no such thing as **off the record.**

So, for example, if he has done your accounts and in your final meeting to approve the accounts you say 'I did a cash job for £5,000 but did not put it through as there is no record of it', this puts your accountant in a difficult position.

He should say that he can't complete the accounts without entering this amount as earnings. Furthermore, he should be suspicious of the records you have been keeping. And worse – he should consider whether to make a money laundering report on you. You can live with your dishonesty but your accountant cannot.

Your accountant might not react to your admission of 'cash' earnings but he will have noted it and may well put it into your accounts without telling you. That way he covers himself and does not make an issue of it with you. You will pay tax on that cash as it is added to your profits – and you might not even realise. All your asking customers for cash during the year was then in vain.

Habit 3: Be a payer

Businesses that use suppliers will deal with their accounts departments and bookkeepers who are generally separated from the person you deal with for the supply of goods. This is the usual organisational division in medium-sized businesses.

Your accountant and his firm are different because the person usually referred to as your accountant or partner is directly responsible for the billing (that is, invoicing/fee notes). Furthermore, any late payers come straight back to him, often with raised eyebrows from other partners. So your accountant will usually be personally responsible for seeing your bill is paid.

He will monitor it, if he is in a small firm, from the day it is issued, or in a larger firm by reporting when it is not paid – say after the first seven days. The amount of time you take to pay will get etched on his mind. If you are habitually late, need reminders and a phone call or two perhaps, then calling you will take on new meanings. In fact speaking to you will be a complete bore because chasing an unpaid invoice is time that cannot be billed and if there is one thing that accountants hate most it is unchargeable time.

So how is this going to affect the advice you are given, you may ask. Well, it is moving you away from the **favoured client** position most dramatically. He will know that, when he gives you advice, he is not likely to get paid for, say, six months. Paying the bill late can indicate you are unhappy with the charges, so he will keep his advice short. He will prefer other clients that pay quickly. Yes – it will affect the advice in the most subtle way.

Pay your bills promptly. This may go against the natural way of business but you need to implement it. Instruct whoever does your payments to do this. You need to gain a reputation with your accountant for prompt payment. That is 'by return'. If you get it into his mind that you are a client who pays bills by return, your advice and service should be moved up in status in the natural order of things. Let's face it, you are going to have to pay it sometime (unless you're disputing it) so pay it **by return** – every time. It does not cost you any more. It may hurt a little at the time, like the dentists' injection, but it will be much better for you in the long run.

Habit 4: Build rapport

Your accountant may not be the most effervescent person. He may be shy and reserved but that does not make him a bad accountant. He may also be a little unforthcoming with his advice until you ask him the right question. Then he suddenly launches into the pros and cons and gives you some well-reasoned advice.

Remember, he is basically a technician who has learnt client relationship skills to a greater or lesser extent. It may be that you have relaxed in the knowledge that you are paying him, and so the effort should be on his part. However, if you want the best in service, don't just leave it at that. Make a conscious effort yourself to develop that rapport and working relationship. I am not saying you mirror his movements in meetings, but if you subconsciously find that's working, then it's a good sign.

Build rapport. Rapport can lead to a better understanding of your affairs which in turn leads to better advice. Some simple guidelines to establishing rapport and productivity are:

Smile when met – be pleased he is giving you a meeting. Try and make some kind of positive comment, even if it is just to compliment him on the coffee or comment on the weather. But after that, don't be too chatty (see below)

Don't talk much – He is giving you advice so let him. He should ask you what he needs to know. Don't carry on the joking after the first comment. The meeting needs to seriously deal with your issues. He does not want irrelevant comments or dialogue.

Kid gloves – Treat his requests for information or action from you as top priority. Act on them the same day if possible. Get a reputation with him for responding by return. Why? Because he will know that when he asks you a question, say by email, he will get a quick answer. So he can keep your file handy pending your response and this saves filing time, remembering time, reminding time – all things your accountant loves. And so he will come to love you.

Use body language to convey honesty – Sitting or standing with open not crossed arms or legs, and proper eye contact are examples of honesty gestures which you should adopt so as not to look shifty.

Don't interrupt – Allow him his train of thought, allow pauses where he can think. You are paying him to think, so let him. In the pause don't just jump in with what is most likely an irrelevant comment.

Habit 5: Speak to the right person

In an accountancy firm there are usually different levels of staff with their own duties. Take a little time to understand the firm and its staff. Previously we went into the different types of staff. Get to know the staff who assist your partner.

For example, suppose the secretary takes in clients' records, keeps track of them, deals with incoming calls, sends out the post and accounts etc. You want to know if they have received your books, or you know your accounts are late and you have to sign them this week to avoid a fine. You feel you must ring up your accountant and check he is on track. Instead, speak to the secretary/receptionist/assistant and put your questions to him/her. You might get 'yes we have them' and 'your accounts were posted out to you yesterday'. That's all you need to know. You have not spoken to the partner and caused a quarter hour unit (say, £40) to be added to your bill in some way. What's more, you have not interrupted your accountant from whatever he was doing to deal with trivia that he knows his staff deal with and he may even have to call that person in to help him answer your question. That could mean a half-hours' charge of £80, as well as a few frustrated sighs from him as he gets back to his work. He will not want to charge his clients for trivia, but he is in business so he usually will.

Should you want to know the current VAT registration threshold, then ask a junior member of the firm (but don't forget the previous advice I gave – **look any question up on *Google* first**). But when you want that serious advice that will have an impact on you financially, go to the partner – your accountant. He does not want to answer simple questions that his secretary/assistant could deal with but he should be pleased to get his teeth into something only he can assist with.

Habit 6: Have an agenda

You need to have thought about what you want. Is it compliance with HMRC or is it to pay the least tax? Your accountant needs to know what you are about, what your goals are, to get things in perspective. He does not want you chopping and changing your mind and he does not want to waste his mind time trying to figure out what you want. Tell him. He needs to get to know you and your needs and avoid confusion. Then he can get quickly on to the task of achieving what you want.

I read about one guy who was incensed, thinking his accountant was no good because he did not advise him to put half his investments in his wife's name (she had no income) so as to get the benefits of personal allowances and lower rates of tax. He claimed his accountant had not advised him properly. He was 'useless' so the client had changed accountant.

The question on his agenda should have been: 'How could I rearrange mine and my family's affairs to pay the least tax?' He should have conveyed that to his accountant in no uncertain terms and not expected his accountant to be all-seeing.

So, set out your agenda in the form of questions. List five that best describe what you want or what you want to avoid.

A sample list might be:

1. I do not want my company to run out of cash.
2. We need to have funds set aside for tax liabilities.
3. Can I maximise tax savings using family, home, cars or other properties?
4. I want to pay no fines at all.

5. I don't mind extra fees if we make savings.

Habit 7: Show your appreciation

When you get the feeling that your accountant has pulled out the stops, gone the extra mile and you have had that useful and suitable advice, you need to consider how you want this to continue. It does need to be a winning situation for your accountant if you want it to be part of a continuous relationship. Part of getting the good advice from your accountant is in making him feel that you understand it is good advice and that it is appreciated. Following on, you need to turn that into some form of practical benefit for him.

This can be:

(a) Fees
(b) Appreciation
(c) Recommendations

Or why not all of them? You could say, 'That's great advice, please send through your bill.' The chances are (save for the bad guys – see later) he will not overstep his mark on the bill. There is no surer way of getting to be that *favoured client* than reminding him to bill. Accountants generally don't actually like preparing bills because they are fiddly and time-consuming and do not contribute to time that can be billed, so they would usually rather do direct client work.

If you can't bring yourself to mention a bill, then a bottle of wine at Christmas and a hamper with the note 'I really appreciate your extra advice over the year' could be a good move. It might cost you £100 but he could save you thousands. He will remember next year and he should try that bit harder.

In addition, he needs to feel that he can charge for special advice. The chances are that the good advice will be given as part and parcel of the time expended on your affairs for which he knows he charges and you pay promptly. But there is an element of 'value' in billing. Top lawyers are keen on this and your accountant will be totally aware of the savings you have made by his advice. If you get a special bill you will most likely have had a great saving. And the path is set for more to follow.

Tell him you are going to recommend him and then when opportune do so. Make sure he knows the client has come from you.

AVOID BEING EGOCENTRIC

You are not the centre of your accountant's world, not even close to it. You are a means of making profit for him or the business. Consequently, it is best for your continued relationship if you avoid displaying traits of egocentrism. Demanding to speak to the partner or insisting on having your demands attended to instantly is a no-no – that is, unless you are happy to be the client from hell who will be subsequently charged treble for every fire-expelling breath.

Try keeping your opinions to yourself; your accountant does not really want (and does not need) to hear them. Prompt him, or tell him the facts of course, and a little of what you favour, but allow him to direct and advise – and listen to what he says.

Avoid sending discourteous, non-addressed emails. Such as

How are we getting on??

sent from your iPhone to a number of people but addressed to no one. This will be met with distaste from professionals.

Unless you want to act like God and are prepared to pay through the nose for it, button up.

I was told a story by a lawyer about one of the most famous long-standing bands of our time. They were UK resident but had received a huge tax demand from the United States IRS. The IRS claimed that the principal songwriter of the last massively successful album had written the songs in the US. There was a huge collection of lawyers and accountants looking glum as this was delivered, gathered in the basement of a leading London law firm. One bright spark at the table said 'Just tell them he didn't write the songs over there.' The senior partner of the law firm said 'There are two problems with that – firstly he doesn't know what day it is and secondly he thinks he's God.'

The accountant's frustration will no doubt get reflected in his fees. The scale of fees will be determined by the relationship and how far upwards they travel. The extra work the accountant may do in chasing or the 'management of expectations' will be compensated by fees.

In the example above the musician that thought he was God was fine because the lawyers and accountants were simply charging more than they could with other clients, making super profits. £10,000 was probably billed somewhere for that time of just 'reading' the letter. God was being charged God fees and he didn't care. To him, someone else paid.

The lyrics of 'Life's Been Good' by *Joe Walsh* of *The Eagles* says proverbially:

I have a mansion, forget the price Ain't never been there they tell me it's nice I live in hotels, tear out the walls I have accountants pay for it all

15

KEEPING DOWN COSTS

So you now have an accountant who does not overcharge and gives you good advice, but you want to keep costs in check. Let's look at some of the ways to do it.

WHY YOU KEEP RECORDS

There are six main reasons why you keep records in your business:

1. You are legally obliged to (tax and company law)
2. You like to know what's going on
3. To correctly deal with receipts and payments
4. To meet your ongoing tax obligations
5. To prepare accounts
6. To keep your accountant's costs down

Clients' record-keeping varies from the impossible to virtually no further work being necessary.

I have had jobs where we had a set of bank statements with no records of what the entries were. In such a case you get the paid cheques from the bank and try and work it out. Expensive.

So the general rule is – the better you keep your records, the lower your accountant's charges should be.

GIVE IN RECORDS IN GOOD TIME

Some clients are habitually late at getting their books in to their accountant. If you leave it until January, you will hit his busiest time of the year. Accountants do not tend to hire temporary staff, so all the strain is on the firms' existing resources. Some firms add a premium for overtime at this time without necessarily telling the client. But clients can react badly to being told they have to pay extra if they leave their books till just before the January deadline. Clever accountants turn this on its head by increasing the general charge and offering a discount if you bring your books in earlier.

You will find things go a lot more smoothly if you allow plenty of time for the preparation – keeping things smooth for your accountant should help keep fees down. And of course you will know your tax liability earlier so will have more time to prepare for it.

Think about asking your accountant when is the best time to give him your books. Some like to have them up to six months in advance and yours may well pick a month when timing is good for him. There is no harm in going with this. One more peg to becoming a **favoured client**. Try and stick to this same month each year.

MAKE SURE RECORDS ARE COMPLETE

One of the most important things to do is to make sure you get everything together in one go when you deliver the books. Records that arrive with essential bits missing can result in aggravation and time wasting.

What happens is this. The job is started by the junior clerk. He finds he is missing essential information. The junior rechecks that he has not mislaid anything and checks his desk and other clients' papers to make sure it's not him at fault. He then writes an email to his senior, who is busy with other work and does not reply. Junior can't carry on job without this information and does not have the authority to contact the client directly. He goes into senior's office. 'Have you got a minute?' he asks. Senior puts aside the job he is doing and learns of the missing information. He sends an email to the partner to ask the client for it.

The partner then, after a few unsuccessful attempts, gets through to the busy client for the extra information. The client hadn't included it because that bit required extra effort, wasn't readily to hand and would have taken time to get – so he had just sent what he had, in the hope that would suffice. The client is somewhat annoyed that he has to be bothered and reluctantly says he will attend to it, but is busy and does not make a note to get it.

It still doesn't come, so another reminder arrives from the accountant. Eventually, the client spends about an hour tediously chasing up this elusive bit of paperwork but gets it. Overjoyed, he rings up partner at 5.30pm and goes into the tale of his efforts, says he's got it and is posting it right now. It arrives about a week later. The staff member who started the job is now out on audit so the job has to be given to someone new. What a load of wasted time throughout the firm – just because the client was lazy.

All in all, this has run up £100 of junior time, £75 of senior time and £200 of partner time in extra time costs – and no actual 'accounts' work has yet been started. Who then should suffer this cost? The accountant will not say to the client that because he did not include that 'interest certificate' (say) in the first place he is being charged an extra £375. He will, frustrated, instead try and claw it back in some way.

My message here is, try and get all the information your accountant is going to need sorted in one go. For example, check you have included a complete set of bank statements with none missing. You think one does not matter but you will only get contacted about it, taking extra time and putting everything on hold. That's to your cost. The same applies to credit card statements, deposit accounts etc. You can't find that elusive certificate of interest? Then call your bank/building society for a duplicate, in advance of being asked.

RESPOND TO REQUESTS

This may be stating the obvious but it surprising how many clients see a request from their accountant as something to get around to in due course. If you delay getting back to him, then the time can rack up. You request will be put to one side in a 'pending tray'. If you get a call, ring straight back; the same with an email requesting information. This will keep your charges down as it's all time: back and forth, missed calls, repeated messages – it all adds up and you're the one who's paying.

Propriety and speed are the elements of a good response. If your accountant has taken the trouble to get in touch, it means he needs this information to complete the work on your affairs. If he could have dealt with it without contacting you, he would have done so. If you do not respond he will ask again... and again. If you still do not respond he could easily put your papers into his bottom drawer and send you an 'on account' bill to wake you up. Getting the job done requires your full co-operation when he needs it.

So, when you get a request, act on it immediately. It does not benefit you to delay a response; in fact it acts against you. If you don't respond in a few days he will have to file your affairs in his pending system, diary your query and recontact you later to boringly ask for the same thing again. It may increase your bill or, if you are on a fixed fee, his annoyance with you, the corollary of which is of course bad service.

COVERING LETTER

It's a good idea to write a short covering letter and send it to the partner with your 'books'. He will mentally log in your books and they will be put into the system. He knows he can just hand your affairs straight over to his staff without any explanation, which can save partner time.

Dear Dave

Please find enclosed my books for the year ended 31 March 20XX as follows:

Cash Book (printed out from computer)

Complete set of bank statements (1 April XX to 31 March XX)

Sales Invoice list and file of invoices

Lever-arch files of purchase invoices
Lists of money owed and outstanding at year end
Credit card statements (the amounts highlighted are business expenses and I have written by the side what they were for)
Copy of HP agreement taken out in year

A couple of things to mention – I sold my BMW 518 car in July for £5,000, which was paid into the bank on 24th June. Sales invoice number 318 dated 6 August for £650 was paid in cash, which I kept. I have put all my home phones and mobiles through the business. My wife has worked with me over the year but not drawn any wages.

Any queries please come straight through to me any time on my mobile 0771234568.

Yours sincerely

In the covering letter, list what you are enclosing and state any exceptional things that may have happened in the year (or say that nothing exceptional has happened).

KEEP GOOD RECORDS

This is pretty obvious: disorganised, messy records will lead to higher accountancy charges. However, this may not increase the bill as much as you think, as we saw from the example of how a bill is made up. But if excess time has been taken on your job by any member of staff, the partner is liable to emphasise the state of your records to justify the bill, simply because it's easy to explain and easy for you to understand. It also sounds much better than saying 'You kept us hanging around and we had to go back and forth for ages while the time just racked up'.

MANAGE YOUR STAFF

Be careful with the way your own staff access your accountant, as this can increase your bill in a hidden way.

Contact is necessary at times, but don't give your chatterbox bookkeeper unlimited access. If they are not aware of the cost of the professional accountant's time, they will make the most of having an advisor on tap to answer their queries about VAT, PAYE, Companies House and other business-related issues.

PAY PROMPTLY

We have emphasised this before in earlier chapters but it's worth repeating: if you become a habitual late payer, inevitably your bill will be increased whenever possible.

OCCASIONALLY QUERY BILL

An occasional comment with reference to the bill can make the point that value matters to you. Such as:

> I really appreciate your service but if there is anything else we can do to make our accounts easier for you just let us know, as we have to be careful on our professional costs.

To keep up your service and advice you do not want to get a reputation as a bill quibbler but showing you are keen to keep costs down should do no harm. After all, your accountant, by his very nature, is cost conscious so he shouldn't blame you for being that way too.

FORGETTING THE BILL

Clients find it very easy to overlook that little bill. Your accountant won't. Each day you do not pay after the first 14 days, you will lose your points on the **favoured client** scale. We had a couple of clients that repeatedly chose to pay their bill a year later when the next year's accounts needed doing. Not a great place to be.

When you see the bill and gulp, do not shove it to one side. Do not think 'I will show him that I think it's a bit steep by delaying payment'. Pay it – and look at these tips for getting your bill down. Don't try and do it by late payment.

LIST OUT BALANCE SHEET ITEMS

At your year end, list the following three main items (if they apply), and any more that may specifically apply to you:

Debtors – who owes you money? Mark any that are bad debts or going that way and add a little note of what steps have been taken to recover your money, and what you think will happen.

Creditors – make a list of money you owe to whom. Revisit that list two months later and mark the date the amounts were paid.

Stock – List out your stock for resale at the year end. Mark any old or obsolete stock that you don't think will sell.

Give these lists to your accountant with your books. They will save him doing this work, or at least give him figures to check. This should save time and therefore *your* money.

MAKE YOUR CALLS PAIN-FREE

If a phone call is absolutely essential then:

> Be polite
>
> Don't waste time talking about irrelevancies
>
> Be patient
>
> Keep to the point

Your accountant is in business – like you – and has the same pressures. Some days he will have planned a number of things he must do for deadlines. Your call interrupts his work *every time*. Be quick, don't waffle. Most importantly, make sure your call is over something pretty important that only he can really answer.

EMAILS OR PHONE CALLS

Do not get your assistant to ring up to get your accountant on the phone unless you want premium charges. It's also impolite.

Short emails will usually be cheaper than a phone call. Use these whenever possible but don't hassle for a reply unless it's very important. Do not send an email in the morning, then call in the afternoon because you have had no reply. Your accountant will have logged your email and when he can deal with it. Give him reasonable time to get back to you or don't use email in the first place – if it's *urgent*, just ring.

Also, don't write long emails full of questions inserted through the paragraphs – that's just rude. If you have a few questions, then set them out in numbered points. If more than four or longish answers are required, suggest a meeting or call instead.

Above all, keep emails **as short as possible**.

If I have clients that send out emails that cc me in and halfway through there is a *Chris – could you check that*, then I make sure they get a full charge. Politeness is an email directly to a person to ask for something, not a line in someone else's that could be easily missed.

ACCOUNTANTS TALKING TO OTHER ACCOUNTANTS

Avoid this wherever possible. They will go into jargon-speak and great detail to make sure they are not slipping up in any way. They will do everything more carefully and thoughtfully, bouncing technical issues off one another like a university debate. While this might be a good thing, as two accountants with a considered, agreed point of view is the best advice you can get, you will be paying one way or another – and this chapter is about keeping costs down.

The exception to this is on the transfer of your affairs to another firm, which should be done free of charge by the outgoing accountant. There are regulations governing how this proceeds, and the costs thereof.

COMPUTERS

Some might think that if you put all the year's transactions into a computer program such as *Sage* or *QuickBooks*, then press the profit and loss button, your accounts will pop out.

If only it were that simple!

You will indeed get a couple of pages of figures in a format that seems familiar, headed up PROFIT AND LOSS. But these can be far away from a final set of accounts, with the profit or loss out by thousands of pounds, or in big companies, hundreds of thousands of pounds.

These first-stage figures out of your computer, or calculated from basic manual records, are often referred to as a trial balance, or TB. This trial balance is basically shoving everything that has happened into a record-keeping system *twice*, then adding up both systems independently and if you get the same answer, *bingo!* You have a balanced trial balance.

Computers are amazingly good at getting it to balance. That's because the program has to shove the second entry somewhere; however, it may not be in the right place. Whether the entries are right or wrong doesn't matter: they add up and that's what counts at this stage. It's the end of year accountant's job to get the entries into the correct place. We often have had to make dozens of correcting entries to trial balances supplied by clients who thought it was all done.

Computer-produced accounts that attempt to balance up a set of defective accounting records can be a massive headache for accounts staff. It could be quicker to start again but they would not be so bold as to say that. Rather, they will labour through the records and leave it to the partner to tell the client why the job has taken twice as long as expected.

FINAL ACCOUNTS

So much work ends up in the final accounts. This is the culmination of bookkeeping/VAT payments throughout the year and the bulk of the accountant's work is at this year end and covers most of the fee.

Since you do not see most of the work that goes on behind the scenes with your affairs, your accountant will make extra efforts to make the final product look good. Your final accounts usually arrive in beautifully bound covers, but they are a menace to file and can easily get sandwiched between other documents and lost.

The cover is only there to give your accountant's showmanship a lift. But it's awkward to file without destroying this cover, so for convenience, rip it off, hole-punch the accounts and file them in a lever-arch file along with all previous years' offerings. Or if you prefer – scan and chuck.

The figures are important, not the covers, and having all the accounts together in one place, year after year, is the most effective way of storing that information for future retrieval. Many clients don't bother with any form of systematic retention and just ask their accountants each time they need a copy. As we are talking about keeping costs down, get your own filing system in order so as not to bother a professional with extra admin that you should do yourself, and get charged.

When the final accounts come, clients make two major mistakes in dealing with signing them off. First, they delay reading the accounts; and then they sign and eventually send them back without paying the bill.

You should be aware that your accountant has been labouring away on your affairs or accounts in the background while you have been getting on with your work or running your business, so it should not come as surprise to receive a wad of documents. Greet them with joy, not despair – because it means that a major bit of work for which *you* are ultimately responsible has been completed .

Go through it when you open the envelope (if it comes when you are rushed don't open it – put it to one side unread). When you read it, deal with it start to finish. 'Don't handle the same piece of paper twice' goes the infamous management consultant's motto, and that certainly applies here.

Realise that you are not necessarily going to understand the small print. When you open the envelope, give it a quick glance and if it seems OK, then sign where indicated. This is your qualified, regulated accountant's work and you should be able to rely on him – so just sign it and send it straight back.

You do not have to understand every word but if something looks blatantly wrong, or you want to ask a question, get on the phone or email the person dealing with your case before signing the accounts and sending them back the same day. And make a habit of that, with the aim of getting your accountant to understand that's the way *you* work. *You* will then stand out with your accountant against all those other tedious clients that he has to chase all the time for everything.

What's more – and very important – enclose a cheque for his fees. You are going to have to pay them sometime, so why not pay early and gain an extra credit. Get this reputation as a quick payer I keep stressing. You will then be elevated in his mind to a client he wants and that, by the law of business-to-business, will be reflected in your service. Win–win.

RECOMMENDATIONS

Accountants love recommendations. Never think they are always busy and don't need them. They are the next best thing to holidays. If you want to recommend a new client, then call your accountant first and ask him if he would like a recommendation. He will most likely perk up and be very pleasant. Slip in, 'Any chance of a discount on fees if I get him over to you?' You might be pleasantly surprised at what he says.

Many accountants attend network events just to get recommendations. They join organisations like BNI (*Business Network International*) where they have to attend a targeted meeting each week at the crack of dawn solely to get new clients. This takes time and effort so your recommendations should be treated like gold.

So if you are happy with your guy, pass his name on. It will certainly move you up the favoured list.

CHANGE ACCOUNTANTS

If you are really not happy with what your accountant is charging, then change. But if it's just the charges you are not happy with and all else is fine, go and speak to the partner. Tell him you are changing accountants as you have been offered the same service elsewhere. You might be surprised just how much he knocks off next year's fee to keep you. Fees have come down, but yours may have stayed at previous levels and there may well be room to move.

EMAIL VOLLEY

Your accountant, who we shall call David, hates getting into an 'email volley' with his client, John. The client tends to forget the earlier advice and asks the same questions but in a different way. Something like this:

> Hi Dave,
>
> Hope you are keeping well and busy!!!
>
> We had a load of trouble with the last tenants on my rental property. They smoked like chimneys and had so many dogs you would not believe. We spent days cleaning up the dog sh** from the garden. I think my nose has now gone numb !!!!

241

Anyway it's looking good and we are taking this void period to do a small extension to give an extra room. Can this be claimed against tax???

Julie send her regards.......xxx

Best

John

***

Dear John,

I am fine thanks, hope you and Julie are prospering.

The taxman does not look favourably on improvements and you cannot generally claim these against the rental. Your extension cannot be claimed against the rental income but keep valid receipts for a claim against any chargeable capital gain at a later date.

Regards

Dave

***

Hi Dave,

We have some new tenants lined up and I just wanted to freshen things up. We will be painting and decorating, can't these be claimed???

Best

John

***

Yes, you can claim for decorating as that's not an improvement but a repair.

***

Dear Dave,

That's great news!!!

What about a new washing machine???

Best John

***

Yes, that's a repair as well.

***

The builder has asked for cash so we will not have a receipt, but I was going to take a before and after photograph to prove it was done !!! Will Mr Taxman be happy with this???

***

John, I will give you a ring to discuss it all – and the money laundering implications. Dave

Points to note

1. Professionals often cancel out previous, repeated emails, clients often don't. This makes filing worse.
2. Dave the accountant is fed up with piecemeal questions. To put an end to the bombardment of emails he suggests a phone call.
3. Remember what we said earlier about money laundering. The worst case scenario is that John's extension could be deemed to be the proceeds of crime due to his collusion with his builder to evade tax. He has cheesed off his accountant who may be more

inclined to labour the money laundering issues than offer a practical solution.

DON'T BE A P.I.T.A. CLIENT

Pain in the assets clients are those that are precisely that. They take up more time than the majority and often produce costing losses.

One practice I knew used to have a vote each year amongst all the staff of the firm. They had to single out which three clients most wanted not to work on.

There are two basic ways to get rid of a client:

Tell them to go, or

Put up their fees so much so that they do.

So if your fees are going up have a careful look at your actions.

PARTNER USE

As we saw earlier, it's the partner's time that pushes up the bill so use him only when necessary. Often other members of the firm do most of the work on your affairs anyway. Your partner is just the figurehead and the giver of that *special* advice.

If you don't want any special advice, then turn down any lunch invitation that may be offered, as you may be charged.

Lunch can work if you use it to get considered answers, so take a list of difficult questions to ask. You may well still get charged for the partner's time at lunch with you, so pump him for answers and let him do the talking. If he knows your business, his throwaway comments could be worth thousands to you, so do not underestimate them.

Being a senior partner is an important and often lucrative job but when things go badly wrong, he has to carry the can and make difficult decisions.

The senior partner's chargeable time to individual clients is generally limited over the year and he is a scarce resource. Consequently, his time has a very high billing quotient per hour, meaning that those clients who use it up get charged extensively. In the larger firms you will get charged for lunch, admin work or time on the golf course. Use these times with care, but remember that the advice you might glean in certain circumstances could be invaluable.

SENIOR PARTNER JOKE

> A man goes into a shop to buy a budgie. 'Yes, we have only those three available in the window but they are special accountancy budgies,' says the shopkeeper.
>
> Amazed, the man says, 'I've never heard of them'.
>
> 'They are incredible,' replies the shopkeeper. 'That yellow one there costs £200 and will do all your bookkeeping. The blue one next to it is £500 and does all that plus your tax return and accounts.'
>
> 'That's fantastic!' says the man. 'Well, how much is the black one at the end?'
>
> 'Oh,' says the shopkeeper, 'he is very special and priced at £2,000.'
>
> '£2,000! What on earth does that one do, then?'
>
> 'Well,' comes the reply, 'not a lot, actually, apart from sleeping – but the other two call him Senior Partner.'

16

BEING PROACTIVE

If you ask clients if they *want* a proactive accountant all will say 'yes'.

While elements of proactivity can exist in the work of an accountant, his day-to-day job is basically reactionary.

He gets a letter from the taxman, he responds. Your accounts or tax return need doing by a deadline, he does them. A client rings up and asks for something, your accountant puts it in hand.

The biggest reactionary task of all is replying to emails. Many accountants think that if they at least keep their emails in check then they are doing fine.

They do not need to have this extra claim to proactivity, it is encapsulated in doing an efficient professional job for their clients. But there can be some add-on's that give 'extra miles'.

What client would say they do not want their accountant to be proactive?

But what is a proactive accountant? They will all champion the claim that they are but can you, as a client, judge? One enterprising accountancy firm bagged the domain name *proactiveaccountants.com.* But does that mean they are? Unlikely, they are probably just the same as most.

Websites are springing up to cash in on the 'proactive accountant' slogan, using this 'proactivity' as some sort of draw to attract businesses. They equate proactivity with extra services such as management information, monthly accounts etc.

Any accountant will provide these if you pay them. They ask: 'Does your accountant really understand your business and direct you to your goals?' inferring that if he does not, you have a bad accountant and should change. The problem is, it can sound convincing to the small businessman. In fact the whole thing is just a sales pitch with little substance.

'Does he just do your year-end accounts and that's it?' they ask you. Well, as it happens, thousands of accountants up and down the country do just that at a cost-effective price.

These sites are playing on the 'grass is greener' effect, making out your accountant should be doing more.

Put simply, he will do more if you ask him – and pay him for it.

So don't be fooled by these claims that your accountant is not as proactive as the ones they can put you onto.

WHAT IS PROACTIVITY?

You could interpret proactivity as:

1. Making things happen
2. Anticipating problems
3. Preventing problems
4. Recommending action in advance

So how does this relate to your accountant?

1. Making things happen

Not exactly his domain. You, the client, make things happen. Your accountant sorts out what you have done. He may tell you that, if you do this or that, then that or this will happen. But that comes usually after you have initiated the question. He is your own personal 'Google'. Say the right words and you will be directed to the answers, not always right but usually pretty close.

As well as this, the firm should have systems in place for triggering off certain actions essential for you, the client, to comply with regulations and deadlines. For example, if you have not sent in your company books for accounts preparation you should be sent a reminder. If you don't get one, it's a bad sign.

2. Anticipating problems

This tends to go hand in hand with prevention.

The big question is to what degree this is done. If you have a personal manager then part of the job may entail this to a large degree. Your accountant who may be on the fringe of your business will not be in this role. You need to anticipate problems in order to prevent them.

You are the one with your foot on the accelerator; your accountant just does the servicing every so often. Just like a car the amount of servicing is up to you. Ignore it and you can get problems. You have to find the right balance between use of the service versus the cost. Just like your car servicing.

3. Preventing problems

Accountants naturally by their work prevent certain problems. If you don't do your tax return you are likely to have fines and nasty letters. Your accountant will remind you to do it and therefore prevents a problem. If your accountant is in a more involved role, such as a quasi-financial director who comes to board meetings, then there is more onus on him professionally to spot issues before they arise.

The biggest of these is probably cashflow. If you have an accountant on the board and suddenly you have no cash or you are trading insolvently (net liabilities as opposed to net assets) then he is basically not doing his job let alone not being proactive enough.

So a certain amount of proactivity comes with the job that is defined by the terms of engagement. Remember (in the Chapter Tied-up) the letter of engagement that every accountant sends out, to cover themselves. In this case, if it does not say they need to do something then there can be no charge against them for not doing that something. It will never ever say they will be 'proactive'.

Interestingly, could the accountants who describe themselves in their advertising as proactive (such as proactiveaccountants.com) be more liable for things going wrong than those who don't?

4. Recommending action in advance

If you see any signs of this, then you may have an exceptional guy. For example, if the tax rates are increasing in April and he contacts you in March to suggest you pay your annual dividend early, then that's truly proactive. He is earning his fees.

I had a client who was selling some private company shares at a time when *George Osborne's* budget of 2016 reduced the top rate of capital gains tax from 28% to 20%. One hour after the budget speech, and that surprise announcement, I emailed my client and told them to delay the sale for three weeks. They saved £750,000.

EXTRA MILES

While we say much is standard for the good accountant some may give more, so let's look at some systems that can be employed in this area.

- Having a system that triggers a letter to clients one month before the year end suggesting a tax-planning meeting
- Letters to clients with bank overdrafts suggesting cashflow forecasts
- Contacting personal tax clients before 5 April suggesting tax saving
- Fixed quotes given in advance without requests
- Timelines given for completion of work
- VAT turnover alert when annual accounts done
- Reviewing company assets
- Examining the director's loan account and discussing entries with you and making suggestions
- Suggesting inheritance tax-planning considerations
- Invitations to seminars e.g. employment laws and HR
- Networking events
- Ad hoc calls and suggested meetings
- Special tax schemes such - as goodwill transfer to limited companies
- Tax-efficient suggestions – such as EIS, VCTs, pensions and ISAs
- Recommendations to the services of others (particularly Financial Advisors) – CAUTION NEEDED: this may not be proactivity but a way to get extra fees.

No accountant will do all of these, but a few is a good sign.

DO YOUR BIT

We have seen what should happen and of course I am going to say it's now up to you to make your accountant extra proactive.

Here are some practices to employ in this direction.

1. Create the time

For your accountant to be extra proactive he needs extra time.

Remember, it's all about time.

If you are constantly late with getting the basics done then his time vanishes on just trying to meet deadlines. When your accounts finally get filed he breathes a sigh of relief that your job is done and goes on to the next client.

You have given him no time to be proactive. Create the time for his mind to focus on *your* affairs.

2. Pay promptly

We have said plenty about this. It applies here too.

3. Be the catalyst

You need to start the ball rolling. Ring up and offer to take him out for lunch or have a special meeting. Again, extra proactivity is part of the favoured treatment (to save you money) – it is not standard – so as before take the initiative. Be a client he wants to do business with.

4. Avoid use of the word

Do not say you want a proactive accountant. He will regard that remark with contempt but not show it.

SAMPLE LETTER FOR MEETING

> Joe Stumble
> 42 The Drive
> London SW19 6SR
>
> Smith, Jones & Co
> Impress House
> Stanburton
> Horseshire ST9 1PQ
>
> 15 December 2001
>
> Dear David,
>
> I wonder if we could have a meeting to look generally at some tax planning on my affairs. As you know, with the formation of the new companies, things are more complex and I feel there are areas that we should be looking at.
>
> I appreciate that this is extra work additional to the usual accounts and tax stuff so I will expect a bill from you for the time that goes into it. I am sure that your fees will be well worth the tax saved.
>
> Yours sincerely

You are saying to him 'send a bill'. This is a delightful request to get from a client, in fact the best request ever you can make to your accountant. It will work wonders in the subconscious.

However, all is not lost on the blank cheque effect. You are covering yourself in saying that his work will be based on time and results. This has three effects:

1. It tells your accountant that you really want action on this front. This means proactive thinking and results.
2. It tells him you are prepared to pay properly for his time (that you value) and the tax saved.
3. It conveys to him that you think his results justify his fees, so you are keeping him on his toes.

Unless he is a crook (and if you have read this book so far you should know by now) he should do a good job and save you money.

NO HOPE FOR SOME

I knew an accountant who had built up his own chartered accountancy practice in London. It made him a good living, was well ordered with about 150 clients. He woke up one day and decided to emigrate to Australia. His clients were astonished as this stable and straight guy must have flipped. He went off with his wife to find a life away from accountancy, away from four walls into those open spaces. I spoke to him six months later and he was working in a Australian accountancy practice doing the same thing but now he was not the boss. He said - 'it's much better, here they play music in the office.' I chuckled as I put the phone down thinking 'Before you ran your own shop and could have put music in at any time'.

He was a 'good' accountant but was not proactive with his own affairs and so maybe would not be with clients'. He was a reactionary, but good at that. Don't expect too much.

17

CHAOS THEORY

The second law of thermodynamics implies that all closed systems will go from a state of *order* to *disorder*. My chaos theory of accountancy says that your accountant, however good, will eventually make mistakes somewhere.

Accountancy is a discipline where it's basically very easy to make mistakes with numbers. Some are small and insignificant, but howlers can lead to a major mis-statement of profit or loss. *Leonardo De Vinci's* pal *Pacioli* recognised this problem and is credited with inventing the system of double entry. The Venetian merchants had realised that, to get things right and to avoid mistakes, they needed to work the numbers over again independently, producing two records, resulting in two answers which must be the same – and if not there must be an error.

However, you can still make many mistakes in the double entry system. Balancing the accounts can give you a false sense of attainment because the accounts can still be full of mis-postings. But the system does work and has stood the test of time up to the present day. It has, however, been watered down to some extent by computers. Accounting computer programs allow you to do double entry but cannot check the accuracy of additions and postings, which defeats the point of the double entry system.

One example of such an error which I came across was where a bookkeeper for a music outfit had labelled 'Fender guitar' as 'security costs' because he thought that this involved a fender built onto the guitar to keep the crowds away. The bookkeeper was not a rock music fan and knew little about the famous pop group he was temping for, let alone the guitars made famous by *Leo Fender*, which are of course a staple feature of rock groups. His mistake meant that fixed assets were understated and security costs were exaggerated. However, the accounts were perfectly balanced.

While the actual preparation of accounts is subject to that double entry rule, certainly helping on the error front, your tax and financial compliance work is not done twice by your accountant. That work is just done the once by a human being who may have had a bad night's sleep, young babies, marriage problems or anything else which might cause his mind to wander or make him wish to get the job done quickly and get home and sort out problems that really matter.

ERRORS

Non-computerised work is therefore prone to omissions and mathematical or accounting errors. Because there is no inbuilt checking system in the actual preparation of tax work, form-filling and compliance, it is inevitable that mistakes will be made.

The most common will be an omission of some kind. Accountants are always on the guard for omissions as they know how easily they can happen.

Often a senior accountant will pick up mistakes made by a junior and correct them, or the partner may spot them in a careful review. Most firms have some form of checking in place, though even these are not foolproof. Very occasionally, the client may spot a mistake, but more often a tax investigation will highlight them, throwing doubt on the firm's competence.

When it is the partner completing the work then his professionalism, self-checking and experience carries him through but, as said, everyone has 'off' days.

SETS OF ACCOUNTS

Mistakes in accounts are usually made by the staff that put them together. This can be juniors (with little experience), seniors, temporary staff, managers or partners. Your accountant has all the normal difficulties in getting competent staff. They have to try them out, they come and go. Often when they are going their care factor goes down. So lurking in those figures will be some howlers. Most go unnoticed but when they come out it looks bad and the partner (who was not at fault) gets the blame. That's fair enough; he is the chief and as such is responsible for the quality of work done.

I have seen final balance sheets that don't even add up – stupid arithmetical mistakes. Some, however, can be intentional. I had a call from a potential client whose unqualified 'accountant' had taken the balance in the bank, equated it to the other side of the balance sheet, and filed it at Companies House to meet the deadline. The client thought their accounts had been done only to discover later that there was another set to be done for HMRC. The potential client did not like the fact that I quoted about £100 more than she was paying already and did not change to us, but it is a good example of the 'getting what you pay for' syndrome.

But, as you will have read in earlier chapters, our system is one in which it is difficult to judge the quality of the service you receive.

CHAOS AT THE TOP

There was a famous case where a firm was asked to advise on the valuation of company shares prior to a sale. A big exercise was done and due processes followed to arrive at a report and a valuation. The report was prepared and eventually went to a senior partner for a final look, before going to the client. He looked at the page that included a summary of the final valuation per share. Adding up the column of figures in a final check, which he had been trained to do in his early days as a clerk, he noticed in amazement that it simply did not add up. In disgust, he crossed out the final figure, corrected it and sent it for printing. He must have cursed about the quality of staff who had let it get to this stage.

As we have said before, it is easy to make mistakes with numbers, especially when you are not using double entry properly. His checking of the addition was an isolated check. What he had done was to add the page number into the column of figures. The figures were in thousands and the consequences were severe. The firm was heavily sued.

HMRC

The most likely outfit to pick up on an accountant's mistakes is HMRC. They raise queries and investigate some aspect of a client's affairs or a set of accounts. Things then can come to light that cast doubt on the accountant's competence, unjustifiably or not.

The accountant may have taken a view on something like entertaining and added back 50% allowing the other half as subsistence. HMRC take the hard line and say it's all disallowable, which in turn knocks out the tax computation and the client now owes more tax. Who is the client going to blame? Not himself obviously, not HMRC, but his accountant. Yet his accountant was just trying to get the best position for his client by getting his tax as low as possible.

These 'add backs' are usually decided by the preparer of accounts. So judgement one way or another here can be beneficial or detrimental. In our own terms that we send out to clients there is a clause that says we may make estimates in your favour that could be challenged by HMRC and if you do not want us to do this let us know. That way we feel we do the best for clients that we can, but without it coming back to bite us if it goes wrong.

I once worked for a firm where a long-serving clerk had to make a judgement on what proportions to add back for personal use of motor expenses, goods taken for own consumption, entertaining and subsistence. The higher the add-back percentage, the more tax the client would pay. Those he liked only got 10% added back; those he was indifferent to about got 40%–50% added back; and those he disliked got 80% added back. No one was any the wiser except for his self-satisfied self.

Often HMRC can delve into a set of accounts in great depth – frequently more so than the accountant did when preparing them. They are not working under commercial pressure like private firms. It is not uncommon for assumptions to be made when preparing accounts, assumptions that can often turn out to be incorrect. When such abnormalities come to light it's the accountant who has egg on his face.

HMRC are now getting their act together on finding discrepancies. Using social media to gather information for investigations.

One method I heard of was HMRC going through properties at the Land Registry and matching owners with the person who pays the council tax. If there is a mismatch, it indicates the property is rented. Then they check the owner's tax return. Hello, they say, no rentals shown – here is an *evader*. Getting your tenant to pay cash for all those years was not the answer.

COMPANIES HOUSE

The other authority that directors of companies come across is Companies House. They are a very efficient operation due to the massive income they get in fines. Their phone is answered so well and all the information is straight to hand. When red letters or warnings come in from Companies House more often than not the client points his first finger at his accountant.

When the registered office is at the client's premises then reminder notices are sent there. If the client does not pass these on to their accountant then things can fall into arrears. Just put all such notices in the post or scan to your accountant. He will then act on them if he needs to. Don't ring him up for something so routine.

If you are late with accounts filing, the penalty regime comes into its own. Although it may not be the accountant's fault they often get to carry the can in the client's eyes. 'He should have told me' or 'It's his job to look after this'. It's so easy and cheap to form a company that the fines seem out of proportion, so the implication is the accountant has got it wrong.

The argument Companies House would fall back on is: 'This is the benefit people must pay for the privilege of limited liability.' So what are they really saying? 'We will let you trade with limited liability and walk away from your creditors as long as you pay us handsomely'? The stupid thing is that clued-up fraudsters can dupe the whole system. They can set up a company for £15, trade for two years with the benefit of limited liability, and then walk away without paying any fines or filing any accounts.

There was a recent case of fraudsters who did just this. They duped people into buying plots of land in Brazil with the easy set-up of a company and were able to waltz off with £5 million from about 300 separate investors. The fraudsters turned out to have recruited *Afghan* refugees as directors, who knew nothing about the fraudulent company.

In 2010, Companies House revealed that 10% of all accounts filed were rejected due to basic errors in regards to formatting. This is most likely the accountant's fault, if you have used one.

Accountants generally use specialist software to produce the statutory accounts. These come out at around 10 pages, for the full accounts, with the push of a button after a trial balance is entered. While they should generally be compliant with the statutory filing requirements, strange entries can quite easily throw them out. The accountant should review them carefully, checking each page before they are finalised. The 'Notes' require special attention as these tend to be customised to the client.

If your accounts are rejected, don't be too harsh on your accountant; it's easy to make errors or typos and, if the software that produces the statutory accounts is not up to scratch, the filed accounts may have all the right figures but be rejected as technically incorrect. Your accountant may still have done a great job on your figures but is caught out on a technicality that for small companies is academic.

Interestingly, many accounts used to face rejection because the balance sheet had not been signed by the client. This is now somewhat old hat due to online filing.

COVER-UPS

As we said back in Chapter 10 on service, your accountant's service will always be claimed to be good. Hence he will not want any of his or his firm's mistakes to come to light. But with all these ways of you getting disillusioned, maybe unjustly, he will want to minimise the situation. He knows you will easily forget the good work he has done and lose the respect you had for him, and you look for other evidence to reinforce your newly found view that he is incompetent.

Some mistakes will be found by the accountant and corrected without telling the client. This can be covered up quite easily inside all the workings that go on. Quite often the client just sees final figures that he 'takes on trust'.

When preparing a year's accounts there is much comparison with the previous year. So much so, that the previous year is often reviewed in detail. Mistakes can often be uncovered during this process. A simple correction in the next year can often solve the problem, but large mistakes with implications should be brought to the attention of the partner, who will then decide on a course of action. Obviously his own interests will prevail when deciding whether he tells the client or not.

Think about the car analogy again.

You take your car to a garage as it keeps cutting out. The garage is unlikely to give a fixed quote as they will say they need to take a look at it. It will cost £25 per hour for labour and cost of any parts used. The car is returned working properly and the bill is for four hours labour plus oil, plugs and distributor: a total of £185. You think, 'Well, to do all that it must take about four hours and it's working great now. That seems fair.'

Unknown to you, when the garage owner opened the bonnet he found that the spark plug cap was off and pushing it on made it all work perfectly. The garage owner considers himself honest, but he is in business and he has to make a profit.

'I have all these overheads,' he thinks, 'I can't find the right staff, and health & safety took up half my day yesterday. It was my years of experience that enabled me to guess to check the plug caps first. That was worth hundreds. If I told him that, I would not be able to get anything towards my overheads – so I just made up a small bill.'

The car owner is none the wiser – in fact he thinks the garage is brilliant, puts his wife's car in for a full check and service, and recommends the guy to all his friends. He continues to use that garage, to regularly service everything with instructions to keep it in tip-top order. Sometimes the bills are quite high – but hey, you can't win 'em all.

Years later, the car owner has a freak car crash and dies – everything points to brake failure. His wife calls their honest, reliable friend at the garage to recover the car and keep it safely for examination. The reliable garage man examines it and reports that the brakes were fine; he expresses his condolences and says he won't charge for the examination and has disposed of the vehicle.

No one is the wiser, except maybe for the garage owner. He had a lucky break with the widow bringing the car back to him, because when he examined it he found that his trainee had forgotten to top up the brake fluid on a recent service.

The garage owner was extremely lucky and took action to protect himself. Your accountant is much better placed to protect himself and even shine through errors.

I knew of one case where a mistake on a client's VAT return caused them to overpay about £10,000. It was discovered some months later by the accountant's staff and on the next return a correction was made generating a refund. The client was overjoyed at the refund and told his friends what a great accountant he had.

In another case I knew of, a freehold property had been left out of a company's accounts for years till it was found out, then cleverly just popped in, using the accountant's magic. The client was none the wiser. No one was adversely effected. The accountant had covered up a serious preparation error in the last ten year's accounts but got away with it.

REACTIONS

When a mistake is brought to the attention of the client, how should he react?

Do not jump to conclusions hastily. Remember, *myside bias* (mentioned earlier) can work in reverse.

Have you never made a mistake with your profession or trade when you were actually doing a pretty good job overall? It can happen even in professions where the utmost care has to be taken – we know surgeons can leave their scalpels inside bodies. That little error could be made by a surgeon, on a bad day, who has carried out years of sheer brilliant work.

So when you uncover a mistake by your accountant do not automatically jump to conclusions, often exaggerated to he is 'useless' or worse.

Judge him by his *reaction* to the error. That is the real test of any professional. They all make mistakes. It's the follow-up that counts.

If you paid too much tax, you can get it back with an error claim. He should explain that and say he will do it for you 'no charge',

If you paid too little, you are rightly going to have to pay up what you should have paid in the first place. You have not lost; but if there is a penalty because of his error, then he should admit it and offer to pay the penalty.

In this situation you are seeing the real mettle of your accountant. Even some good ones will try and cover up their errors. They know that admission of an error could be taken very badly by their client so that they just go to another firm.

It's human nature not to admit mistakes unless you have to. Cover-ups happen all the time, so don't assign your accountant superhuman properties. He will not naturally put his hands up, although if he does, he's exceptional, so stay with him.

Human slip-ups need to be forgiven as long as they are not repetitive and especially if admitted and compensated. Judge him by his reaction to the error.

TAX RETURNS

Despite our 'accountants' bad days', mistakes on tax returns, usually omissions, often boil down to the client not giving, let's say, 'full and frank disclosure' or forgetting something or assuming their accountant knew all about it. There is a tendency with some clients to be economical with information resulting in possible lower tax; yet holding on to an excuse like 'I told you so and so and assumed that was okay'.

Most accountants are wary about this and the omissions, so they cover themselves by tying the client down for information. This can take the form of a letter, questionnaire or sometimes a meeting.

My firm sends to all clients on 6 April each year the following questionnaire (shown here without the answers section).

*Please complete this form promptly so that we can
complete your personal tax return in the most efficient
and cost effective way.
All the information relates to
 the tax year 6th April xxxx to 5th April xxxx.*

EMPLOYMENT &	*Give details of any new businesses started*
PENSIONS	*in year*
RECEIVED	*(ongoing business we already know about)*
	List all employments/benefits in kind/pension
	received in year
	Enclose all P60's / P45's / P11(D)'s
BENEFITS	
RECEIVED	*Give details of any state benefits received*
	Please provide names and dates of birth
CHILD BENEFIT	*of all children*
	Please provide details of any child benefit
	received during the year
	*Give details of **all** bank and building*
INTEREST	*society interest*
RECEIVED	*Specify where a/c's are in joint names*
	*(assumed to be paid **net** of tax unless stated)*
	Give details of any received
DIVIDENDS,	
OR TRUST	
INCOME	
RENTS	*Give details of any rental income received*
RECEIVED	
CAPITAL GAINS	*Give details of any assets sold,*
	any enhancement costs, dates etc.
DONATIONS &	*Give details of any gifts made to charity*
GIFTS	*State if made under charitable covenants*
PENSION	*Give details of company and amounts paid*
PAYMENTS	*in tax year*
	*(assumed to be paid **net** of tax unless stated)*
OVERSEAS	*Give full details of all overseas income,*
ASSETS	*any assets held such as property,*
AND INCOME	*bank accounts, shares etc.*
COMPANY	*Please list any company directorships*
DIRECTORS	
CONTACT	*To confirm details could you please advise*
DETAILS	*– Telephone number*
	– E-mail address

So that should solve the matter. The problem is that not everyone completes it. There are some clients who feel they are above such forms. They have the attitude that their accountant knows all about their affairs so they do not need to do anything themselves. The onus then comes back to the accountant – does he push for its completion or does he do it a different way? Surprise, surprise – the answer lies in how much he is getting paid. If the fee is normal he will usually insist on completion. If extra fees can be charged by going to see the client, sitting down with them and completing it as he is asking questions, then he may do it that way. The client feels they are getting some special service and the accountant puts a few hundred pounds on the bill.

TAXOPHOBIA

It is suggested by academics that there is a phenomenon known as 'tax aversion', where people look at tax differently to other expenses. They are prepared to go to great lengths not to pay tax and this means they will self-justify all sorts of actions including those that are actually illegal. This is not just a textbook case, it is the norm, as I can vouch for from my many years of dealing with clients. They all want to go to every practical level possible to avoid taxes.

A tax system should by its nature be fair – and in a way our one in the UK is, because the same rules apply to everybody. But then when we come to its practical application it falls down. The richest and the multi-nationals get out of paying tax by hiring tax experts and lawyers to scheme away their millions. Using overseas trusts, tax havens, concocted interest charges, complex planning and considerable law bending, they get away with it.

Unfortunately, this means that the people in the middle – that is, those on PAYE and running small businesses, keeping their foot constantly on the accelerator – pay more than their fair share. The trouble is they are too busy working to pay their tax and other bills to do much complaining.

Accountants know this and will be sympathetic to their plight, and, with moral fortitude, will want their clients to pay the least amount of tax possible, always keeping on the right side of the law but taking every opportunity available to reduce the tax burden.

In 2006, the *Guardian* found that the world's three biggest banana companies did nearly $750m worth of business in Britain but paid only $235,000 in taxes between them. That is just a tiny 0.3% of turnover. Google has recently been outed as paying 3% of turnover in corporation tax.

What the big companies do is set up a head office in a tax haven, base their operations there and charge their own companies in the UK. The tax haven company charges for management services, branding, promotion, interest on loans at above market rates – all things that are deductible, bringing their profits in a high-tax nation (i.e. the UK) down to negligible levels. *Google, Amazon* and *Starbucks* have brought these practices into the public domain.

There is nothing to stop the small UK business doing this, but do not tell your accountant that you are inflating prices. What you are doing is in fact fraud and breaches the tax legislation and money laundering regulations. While the big companies seem to get away with it, they only do it with armies of highly trained tax accountants checking they are not stepping over the line. These people cover all the angles, examining the law with the detail of a QC. Don't think you can do the same: you will be easy meat to the UK HMRC who can throw the anti-avoidance and transfer pricing legislation straight at you – and you will wonder what has hit you.

There was a BBC TV programme in 2016 about some villagers in *Crickhowell, Wales* who banded together to set up offshore centres akin to the mammoth digital tax avoiders on everyone's lips. It was doomed to failure from the start.

18

BAD GUYS

A bad accountant is going to let you down in one of these main areas:

Fees – by overcharging

Service – you can never can get hold of him and he does not call back promptly

Compromise – he will in some way compromise his work with you, for example, getting you to buy into some scheme

Advice – he tells you to do something that is unnecessary or wrong

Tax saving – he tells you to pay more tax than you should and falls short on his job of getting you the best position

HMRC – he gets you into unnecessary trouble

Fraud – he pushes you into fraudulent areas or worse carries them out himself

TAKING TOO LONG

In any business, balancing service with availability of staff is always an issue. Accountants can't afford to have staff sitting around waiting for jobs to arrive and then work on them immediately. In any busy accountants office, accounts will be waiting to be done. Then suddenly the client pops up

271

who has left everything till the deadline and he wants to jump the backlog. If you are a dutiful client you may suffer some time delays due to these queue-jumpers. Don't be too hard on your accountant if it takes a couple of months.

Accountants will get peaks and troughs. Many year ends are 31 March or 31 December and everybody has to work to the 5 April tax year. January is the worst time for tax accountants, as 31 January is the tax return deadline. You would be surprised how many clients bring their books in in the last week thinking they have been really conscientious and made the deadline without a thought for the accountant who might have 50 tax returns to do in that last week.

The larger firms will operate a year planner where staff are allocated in advance to jobs in a specified time frame. This is good in theory – until a client says at the last minute they are not ready or a particular staff member falls ill.

So with this in mind judge if your accountant has taken too long. Some do. I knew a partner of a small firm who discovered a client's tax return that had been in his partner's brief case for six months waiting to be done. Size up your time delay carefully.

SUDDDEN TAX BILLS

Nine times out of ten, an unexpected tax bill will be your own fault. But there is the one in ten that is your accountant's fault.

The key point is, if you are ahead with getting your accounts in to your accountant, you should not get surprise tax bills. Your accountant should let you know in advance (maybe three to six months) what you need to pay and when. One advanced trick (saved for **favoured clients**) is to do your accounts early but not submit them until the deadline. Subsequent events can change the figures to your advantage but this way you always know your maximum tax liability.

However, if your accountant has had your complete records for some time and all your tax return information, then to suddenly get told your tax in the last week or so before payment is a bad sign.

NOT FOLLOWING INSTRUCTIONS

I have heard people say 'My accountant has not done what I asked.' This can happen. You can take precautions to prevent this by giving important instructions in a letter or by email.

Remember, your accountant will not blindly follow all instructions, as there are certain professional ways of dealing with matters which will override your instructions if they conflict.

Conversely, he may do certain things that seem strange but this may boil down to professional obligations. If you query why something has been done in a particular way, you will usually find there is a valid reason for what he's done.

A FAILED ACCOUNTANT

One of the first famous comedians to get prosecuted in the UK was *Ken Dodd* when the Revenue were gunning for a public example of tax avoidance. In the trial it was found that *Dodd* had the classic cash in a suitcase in his attic which amounted to some £336,000 in notes. When the judge asked him what it felt like to have that much cash (remember that was equivalent to well over a million now) he quipped 'the notes are very light my Lord'. Just like the afore-mentioned football manager in my first chapter, *Doddy* was acquitted. The Revenue had failed again even when they had damning evidence. Juries like celebrities, the Revenue were just starting to learn. According to *Wikipedia*, after the trial, he would introduce his comedy act with 'Good evening, my name is *Kenneth Arthur Dodd*, singer, photographic playboy and failed accountant'.

PwC TOP ADVISORS?

The case of country singer *Willie Nelson* is classic for the enormous amounts involved and the 'top' accountants too. His accountant *PwC* had got him involved in various dubious tax schemes. It all ended up with him owing some $16.7 million in back taxes to IRS. The IRS seized his property and when he couldn't come up with the money, sent all his possessions to auction. The only thing he salvaged was his guitar (no doubt his favourite). *Nelson* received an undisclosed settlement from *PwC* to settle claims against them that they had involved him in bad tax shelters.

CREATIVE ACCOUNTING

There can, however, be bad eggs who carry on undetected, not doing too much damage to one client but just feathering their own nest with deception and skill.

An unregulated accountant I came across was championed by his 200 clients. They thought he was a great choice and used to recommend him well. No one really questioned his qualifications. He had built up his practice by recommendation. He worked on his own with one secretary and made a habit of travelling to visit his clients personally, even the small ones. He drove a large convertible and knew South London better than the cab drivers.

A routine HMRC investigation caught the attention of the Revenue inspector, who felt all was not quite right with the answers he was getting to his questions. He looked more deeply into the accounts and found so many errors his conclusion was the whole accounts had been 'fudged'.

Fudged is an accountancy term for getting something to balance when things do not add up. Of course there are different degrees of fudging. In this case the fudging was absolute. The whole accounts were made up.

What our unregulated accountant did was to start with the profit he wanted and then work backwards, estimating the expenses and then in a wonderful display of creative accounting, conjure up a balance sheet out of thin air. He was sufficiently experienced to do it quite well. He wouldn't need to open or examine his client's books, even though they dutifully delivered them to him, and he then gave them back as if he had worked on them. The clients got the profit they wanted and then the tax charge they expected. He billed them as if he had done loads of work, thus making a great profit. He was a PR genius.

While that example may be extreme, it is true and I came across it by chance. What is really shocking is that he had been getting away with it for almost 30 years. Remember, the clients thought he was great. For years, clients thought the American financier *Bernie Madoff* was great, too – until his $65 million fraud came to light.

You might think your accountant is great. If so, just analyse just why you think that.

EGGS IN ONE BASKET

Some accountants have been forward in remote-access bookkeeping. This new use of technology is appealing and programs like *Xero* are rapidly expanding. If you use a system operated by your accountant where all your prime records go through him, you create a difficult situation if something goes awry in your relationship.

I once took over a client who had done just that. The accountant had sent out bills of more than £10,000, which the client disputed and refused to pay. Solicitor's letters started. The accountant pulled the plug on the records. The client could not get access and therefore, with no past data, could not do their VAT and tax returns – and were plunged into insolvency. The accountant had actually shot himself in the foot with the insolvency issue; but when fees become an issue it all gets very emotional.

Your financial records are important matters for which you are legally responsible to the authorities. Do not hand all your records over to a third party whose main concern is maximising the money they get.

It all very well until things go wrong; for instance:

(a) If you fall out with your accountant (and many do), he can send you a bill and unless paid, refuse to release all your software. This can have disastrous consequences. I knew of one client whose company went under because of this.

(b) He can simply go out of business. You might not be able to get hold of him or have access to your records.

(c) The firm can have a computer malfunction and lose your data. We all know computers are fallible.

(d) He can get behind with his/your work. He is not going to tell you it's all piling up and not being processed.

(e) The software company he used goes out of business. It's not his fault but you suffer.

You are losing control of your records, which are essential to you. It's a bit like handing the total build and design of your house over to a builder off the street – okay until it goes wrong. Accountants are still learning with these systems, still seeking the best 'back-up' policies. They are themselves in a commercial jungle. They are trained in accounts not IT professionals – so beware. Cloud accounting is becoming ever more popular, I am just urging a bit of caution.

DETECTION DIFFICULTIES

With the exception of service issues, it is virtually impossible for you, as the client, to assess the other failings. It is very difficult to know you are getting a bad deal.

Little things may start to promote doubts, then a big error might confirm it, but usually the signs are disguised. The client philosophy tends to be 'better the devil you know' and changing accountants is a hassle, so you soldier on in ignorance, hoping things will improve.

There are indeed some high-profile cases where highly recommended professionals have walked off into the sunset with millions of pounds of clients' funds, but they are rare. In all professions there is the odd rotten apple. You are usually protected from negligence, fraud or crime if you are a client of a well-regulated firm because they will be covered by insurance. If a particular partner goes AWOL, you should be covered.

Many choose larger firms for that reason and are prepared to pay the premium for it, but regulated accountants right down to the sole practitioner are all subject to annual checks that they carry insurance and are doing the basics. That's where recommendations come in. If you know someone has been using the same guy for 15 years then that is a far better bet than picking someone from the internet, whatever their claims and glowing testimonials.

BAD ADVICE

Because it's so difficult to judge, bad advice can go unnoticed and furthermore it can be mistaken for good advice. How can you know if your advice is good or bad?

You have two choices:

1. Go with it in the faith that your guy is right, or
2. Analyse it yourself, think about what he is advising, *Google* it, put the question on the accounting website *accountingweb.co.uk* which is full of accountants freely giving answers to 'taxing' questions.

It can be years later when it comes to light that you should have done this or not done that and you would have been tax richer. You then find out you were advised wrongly. It may be your accountant was simply wrong at the time but there can be other reasons. He was not given the full information – did he ask all the right questions? Or maybe time has changed matters and it is only with hindsight that the best advice can be seen.

I have often heard the excuse 'I had bad advice' as the reason for some business/personal financial decision that turned out wrong. But really 'bad advice' is usually quite complicated and has to be examined by another professional in the same discipline to draw a proper conclusion. So, if your new accountant says you had 'bad advice', then that is probably the case.

COVER-UP's

It is quite easy for accountants to cover up bad advice and work. Most errors will go completely undetected. If there is no need to tell the client then they will not do so.

Errors start with the clerks preparing accounts and can go all the way to the top. In my early days as a trainee accountant I worked in a room with others, all preparing clients' accounts. I remember the banter across the room about a new accounts clerk doing a year-end accounts job for the first time.

What did John do on this client last year? – The guy has fudged the bank, it did not balance. I will have to fudge it again this year to make it agree. Who does he work for now?

No client will be told they had to 'fudge' the bank reconciliation. The bank is a pretty basic thing for staff to get right.

FEELGOOD FACTOR

Most accountants in practice have developed PR skills to manage 'client expectations'. Things that may be the norm for reasonably proficient accountants will be trumpeted as special by the PR expert who wants to exaggerate his 'greatness' with his clients. He will seek to impress his clients at the easiest opportunity, leaving them with the impression that he is not just an ordinary accountant but super-good. You just won't know any better because you have nothing to compare it with. He knows that and also he knows your 'level' of knowledge and can tailor his patter to that 'level'. 'Perception is reality', as the PR men say, and that carefully crafted perception makes them appear to be *good*.

Accountants want happy clients. Both good and bad accountants.

The good ones will strive with your affairs, fighting your corner, telling you the soundest things to do.

The bad ones will focus on your feelgood factor. Managing your expectations. Making the most of ordinary savings. If they see you as superficially satisfied then their job is done. No time needed for further extras if you are in that feelgood place already. And if you are there already and they can convince you you need some extra work doing, then out comes a new bill. These are the most dangerous accountants.

TRAITS OF BAD SERVICE

- Not returning calls or emails within a reasonable time. Two days for calls, three days for emails, are reasonable limits.
- Keeping you waiting on appointments.
- Direct calls or visits from tax inspectors, other than for PAYE queries or arrears. Your accountant should have anticipated these and stopped them.
- Getting your accounts in late or taking a long time to do them when he has all the information.
- Failing to warn you that a Companies House or HMRC fine is being issued against you.
- Passing you to a junior when you ask to speak to the partner.
- Paying more tax than you were told.
- Not advising you in advance when you have a tax bill.
- Accountant not qualified or regulated but makes out he is.
- Don't hear for ages, then out of the blue get a bill in the post.
- Losing your records.
- Always having an excuse.

ASSOCIATED PROFESSIONALS

If you are unfortunate enough to have struck on a bad accountant, be wary of his associates, particularly financial advisors.

I was once involved with a famous pop group who had picked a really bad four-partner firm of chartered accountants that eventually went bankrupt. But these accountants had set up the band with pension schemes and received, in today's money, about £3 million in commissions.

Someone once likened a financial advisor to a man outside a betting shop asking you for money to put on a horse. I would take it a stage further. It's like giving your money to a smartly dressed guy who puts 80% on any old horse running in five years' time. He claims you have a sure winner coming up and in the meantime you should be putting some other money in a safe place he will recommend for the even more distant future and your family.

ROGUES

While many accountants will, with considered self-justification, seek to maximise their fees for work which *they* consider invaluable, there are a few accountants who will set out to fleece you for whatever they can. Luckily they are rare – but, like pickpockets, you need to look out for them and be slightly on your guard.

These rogue guys, as well as having convinced you they are the best, will be looking to sell you all the 'extras' they can, whether you need them or not. The danger is in being talked into something you don't need, or is inappropriate or costly, by the accountant you hold in some esteem.

These services could be pensions, life assurances (through an affiliated IFA), tax savings schemes, and management accounts (when not needed).

Then there is tax investigation insurance. This sounds too good to be true but the comfort it provides is worth a mere £20 a month. You don't read the small print or even consider it. If you did you might see that:

- It just covers accountant's basic fees, nothing else.
- It is void if you have been dishonest in any way.
- It actually protects the accountant more than you.

- The accountant can rake in a good commission if he farms it out to all clients.
- On average, only 2 or 3% of clients get investigated.

EVERYONE HAS THEIR PRICE

A Mafia godfather finds out that his accountant has cheated him out of $10 million. His accountant is deaf and dumb – the reason he got the job in the first place. It was assumed that a deaf and dumb accountant would not hear anything that he might have to testify about in court.

When the godfather goes to confront the accountant about his missing $10 million, he brings along his long-standing attorney, who knows sign language.

The godfather tells the lawyer, 'Ask him where I can find 10 million bucks he embezzled from me.'

The attorney, using sign language, asks the accountant where the money is. The accountant signs back, 'I don't know what you are talking about.'

The attorney tells the godfather, 'He says he doesn't know what you're talking about.'

The godfather pulls out a pistol, puts it to the accountant's temple and says, 'Ask him again!'

The attorney signs to the accountant, 'He'll kill you if you don't tell him!'

The accountant signs back, 'OK! OK! You win! The money is in a brown briefcase, buried behind the shed in my cousin Enzo's backyard in Queens!'

The godfather asks the attorney: 'Well, what'd he say?'

The attorney replies, 'He says you don't have the guts to pull the trigger.'

19

TROUBLESHOOTING

If you feel the fees are on the high side, then before an actual complaint try asking for a review. A simple polite email or letter such as:

> *Dear Dave,*
>
> *Over the past few years my turnover has declined and the business has slimmed down. My costs have fallen, as has my income – except for my accountancy charges, which have remained at the same level.*
>
> *Would it be possible for you to review these fees and see if savings can be made?*
>
> *Thank you once again and I wish you and your staff the very best.*
>
> *Yours sincerely*
>
> *Joe Stumble*

What response might you expect to this request? No accountant likes to reduce fees or be accused of overcharging, even in the most subtle way. He is actually in a difficult position. If he agrees to reduce them then it really is saying that he has been overcharging. If he does not do so he is quite likely to lose a client.

One reaction might be to suggest that to get to a reduced fee you could make some changes. He might suggest you keep better records, get them to him at his fallow time, do your own VAT, stop being a limited company and change to a sole trader, not have a visit each year, have your affairs dealt with by a more junior member. A good response might be:

> *Let us make it right for you by agreeing a fee over the next few years that can't be beaten. What would you say to a 25% reduction?*

COMPLAINING – YOUR FEES BILL

Sometimes it has to be done. Initially, keep an open mind as your accountant may have done a lot of work behind the scenes of which you were unaware, so give him a chance to explain. But it's not an easy task so let's try and make it less painful.

If you are unhappy with the amount charged, write **promptly** on receiving the bill along the lines of:

> *Dear Dave,*
>
> *Thank you for the work done this last year and for sending my accounts. I just received your latest bill and was a little surprised that it was so large. Perhaps you have done work I was unaware of. I would be grateful if you could review it and let me have a breakdown of the time that has gone into our affairs over the period and the charge-out rates used. I am quite happy to come in and discuss the charges if that would assist.*
>
> *I await hearing from you.*
>
> *With best regards*
>
> *Joe*

A letter or email is probably better than a phone call. This is because you will be interrupting him on a job – not the best time for a complaint. Also the accountant will need time to look at the file, see what the time costs were and how the bill was calculated. It is not unheard of for an accountant to guess the bill. I knew one partner who used to gauge the bill on the weight of the file. He would hold out the file in his hand as if weighing it and say: 'That's about £2,000 – bill that.' This was most unprofessional but he got away with it back then.

The letter shows the accountant that you are price conscious – some clients are not. It puts the ball in his court to give you the proper information. As we said before, bills are usually devoid of breakdowns.

Nine times out of ten there will be room in the accountant's bill for a reasonable discount.

COMPLAINING – YOUR SERVICE

The most common complaint about service is **speed**. Speed of doing accounts, giving you your tax liability or returning calls/emails. Remember, accountants have a balancing act to undertake. They cannot have staff hanging around just waiting for your queries. They will be occupied on other work and have work on their to-do list. But your accountant must have a basic set of competency in this area. You can expect a reasonable level of response and falling below that means you should be looking more carefully at his work. We covered some response times in earlier chapters.

If you are displeased, then a first stab might be a throwaway comment. 'I thought you took quite a long time to get my accounts back,' casually remarked, should be noted. 'Are you quite sure this has been checked right through?' can get some reaction without animosity; it shows you are on the ball and aware that errors may be made, so he will be extra cautious with your file.

But then serious lack of attention might prompt you to write a note. You need to be specific and accurate, such as:

> Dear David,
>
> I have very much appreciated your help and advice over past years but have been upset by some of the recent service. In August, I sent you my accounts to prepare, and was also expecting the completion of my tax return for this last year. It is now some six months on and I have not heard from you. I did telephone your assistant and left a message but heard nothing back.
>
> I know that I am due to pay my tax in two weeks and I have no idea how much I have to pay.
>
> Could you please let me know what's happening?
>
> Yours sincerely
>
> Joe Stumble

Well you have now clearly let the cat out of the bag. But this is the plan and now your judgement comes with his response. This is where you will find out his real worth as your accountant. Let's consider possible responses:

1. I am really sorry. It has been an unusually busy year for me, so as a gesture of good faith I will not charge you for this year and your accounts will be done for the deadline. You should provide about £5,000 for your tax, based on about the same profits as last year. [He did an approximate calculation in about 10 minutes.]
2. We have been waiting for information from you, as per the letter we sent you in September. [This was never received by Joe].

3. Sorry, we will do them by the end of the week.
4. No response.
5. We sent these out to you last month and can only assume you did not receive them, so we will send another duplicate set out to you.

Now, which response would you like? If you have doubts about the honesty of 2 or 5 you should change accountants. If you get 4 you should change accountants. If you get 1 then stay with him. Now for 3 you are in a quandary, go on your hunch.

COMPLAINING – YOUR ADVICE

How on earth do you know how good your advice is? This is the million-dollar question. You are not really going to be able to access an individual piece of advice unless an error in it jumps out and bites you. But use your intuition.

Look again at Chapter 8 onwards and see how you think your guy measures up. Take the *Good or Bad quiz* at the end of this book and see what he scores. If you have tried the methods in Chapter 14 and it still seems hopeless then changing may be your only route.

NOT PAYING THE BILL

This is not a good policy. The accountant will probably send you some reminders and then if no response call you. You then have to explain why you are not paying it and why you have not raised any complaint. You may find there is a term in the letter of engagement (remember that?) saying that you agreed to raise any concern with the bill within 21 days. It's now two months on, oops.

Things could lead on to a statutory demand or County Court action by the firm. If the accountant can show in court that you had a letter of engagement in place, his time had been properly recorded and the charge-out rates were reasonable, then you will most likely lose unless you can show some glaring error like the balance sheet not adding up.

GETTING FEES BACK

You will meet great resistance in trying to get any fees paid back. Accountants hate writing out cheques and they will do everything but that one thing if humanly possible. Requests to them relying on their good nature are unlikely to produce results.

I had that client who paid extra fees to his former accountants for specialist tax advice. The accountant then forgot to implement the advice. My client asked for his extra fees back and the accountant just laughed.

COMPLAINTS TO A PROFESSIONAL BODY

This is only possible if your accountant is regulated. If he is not a member of one of the bodies that discipline their members then there is nobody to grouch to.

This action is feared by your accountant, especially if there is a valid complaint. It is important to realise that the governing bodies do not handle complaints about the level of fees. They specifically exclude this, not regarding it as a 'professional complaint' type matter. It is a contractual issue between two parties and there are conventional ways to sort it out. However, they do run a fee mediation scheme which actually works very well. They will look at both sides of the argument and, if they feel that the accountant has overcharged, will make persuasive attempts to get him to compromise and reduce the charge. Often that accountant is now the ex-accountant and relationships have broken down, but he will follow the specific recommendations of his professional body.

The most serious actions are those of professional conduct complaints. A valid complaint of this nature will launch an investigation by the professional body, which can have serious outcomes for the practitioner.

Some examples of professional misconduct would be:

- Not replying to letters
- Not following tax return guidelines
- Not having insurance
- Not handing over your books and files
- Conflicts of interest

It may be that the accountant's action encompasses professional misconduct and negligence. Your negligence claim is a legal matter and one for his insurance company to handle. Obviously, a professional misconduct report would act evidentially in your claim against him.

WHO IS LIABLE TO HMRC?

You personally are ultimately responsible for the correct completion of your tax returns to HMRC. Any task completed by an agent you employ is down to you. HM taxman will look to you for the full tax, interest and penalties that are due. If they can see that you are totally innocent then they should be sympathetic but will still look to you for all the financial remedies. No bills will ever be levied on your accountant in respect of your affairs. You will not be able to avoid the tax due or the interest; there may, however, be some mitigation of the penalty that is charged for carelessness. HMRC state the following guideline in respect of this situation:

A return may be inaccurate because someone acting on behalf of a taxpayer, like a tax advisor, has failed to take reasonable care. It is however, the taxpayer who is responsible for the accuracy of the return, and they may still be charged a penalty. No penalty would be due if the person can show that they took reasonable care to ensure that the return was accurate.

Reasonable care in this context would include:

- Appointing an agent competent to deal with their affairs
- Giving the agent all the relevant information
- Checking the return as far as they could, before it was submitted

You may therefore be able to avoid the penalty on these grounds – but only the penalty, not the tax or interest. Show clear evidence (emails for example) that you have done all the above three points and you stand a good chance of it being waived.

INDEMITY INSURANCE

All regulated accountants are required to have professional indemnity insurance. This covers all aspects of professional negligence. Some examples of claims are:

- Failure to spot fraud when auditing company accounts
- Not properly advising on tax payments
- Overvaluing company assets and shares
- Selling bad tax avoidance schemes

If you claim negligence and loss, your accountant has a duty to inform his insurer of a 'potential claim'. They do not like doing this as it can affect next year's premium. Consequently you may get a letter saying they don't accept that there is any loss and therefore it is not a notifiable loss.

It should be remembered that you have to have some actual *loss* for there to be monetary compensation. If your accountant just makes a mistake in your tax calculation –

let's say, asking you to pay £1,000 instead of £100,000 on the day your tax is due and you later get a bill for the outstanding £99,000 in tax – you cannot claim this as you should have paid it then anyway. You could, however, claim from him any fine levied and any extra interest that you have suffered as a result.

LEGAL ACTION

This is definitely a last resort. Don't embark on this without first exhausting the other routes outlined above The accountant will probably defend out of principle and any court experience can be time-consuming, costly, stressful and daunting.

Your easiest route is the online small claims court. It's actually quite simple to do and, once you have tried it, it can become a useful tool in your business armoury. A simple summons might well promote a negotiated settlement and, additionally, you will have the court pushing for the two parties to settle. Just remember that your accountant is probably more experienced with court matters than you. If he has been holding out he will most likely put in a robust defence and you could be in for a fight.

HOW TO MAKE A SMALL CLAIM

Search for money claims online in Google which will point you to the government online service. You have to register with your details then you simply follow the instructions provided. There is a small fee to pay based on the amount claimed. Guidance notes are provided and you should be able to complete the claim in quite a short time. You may also or alternatively choose to consult a solicitor about your claim, especially if you think it might be quite a high-value one.

REFUSING TO FORWARD INFORMATION

This usually only happens in one case – outstanding fees. What happens is this. Your old accountant gets a letter from your new accountant. He feels dumped, and his only compensation is to send a bill bringing all his time up to date. This will most likely be the maximum he can bill you for. If you do not settle this, or in fact have old, unpaid bills, then the response to your new accountant is likely to be along the lines of:

> *Thank you for your letter. We have no professional objections to you acting for Mr X. We will be happy to provide transfer information when our fees are settled.*

Your new accountant may advise you to settle the bill, if it is reasonable. But if you are incensed and absolutely do not want to, it is not the end of the world as far as information is concerned. All your tax details can be got from the tax office by your new accountants.

Formal company statutory books are legally obliged to be kept at the company's Registered Office, which you should change, if necessary.

You should have copies of your accounts, but complications occur when breakdowns are needed of figures in the accounts – such as debtors, creditors and fixed assets – and these have been done by your accountants. Also, if you have given in your books for the next year to be done and you need them back a *lien* can extend over them.

A sneaky trick is to get your books back *then* tell him he is fired.

LIENS

A lien is a legal term meaning that something of yours may not be released until a bill is paid – like your garage may not give you your car back until you have paid for the service. They are legally entitled to do this if certain conditions are fulfilled.

In the case of unpaid fees, the accountant can exercise a lien over certain of your items, as permitted by law and his professional guidelines. These liens are frowned upon by his professional body but can be exercised in certain circumstances. They can even extend to refunds and monies received on your behalf, but it is most unusual for liens in this circumstance, as the accountant usually has in place authorisation to deduct his fees out of monies (refunds) received.

Liens can only be levied on books and records, or anything else for that matter, that have come into the accountant's possession under the ordinary course of business, although they do not extend to company statutory books.

CHANGING ACCOUNTANTS

When you have finally decided that your guy cannot be made into a good accountant, that really he is useless, fraudulent or any one of labels we have for a bad accountant, then change has to come.

There are four main situations that prompt a change:

- You could meet someone who could be a better choice than your current accountant.
- Your existing guy has served you well for many years but lately seems less interested in you.
- You have decided your accountants are incompetent or dislikeable.
- You are moving because of price.

One or all of these can lead to your decision to change accountants.

You may well have a certain loyalty built up and really don't want to change but feel you have no choice. The change process between regulated accountants has been made as easy as possible, so there should be nothing to stand in your way.

If you go to the potential new accountant and explain the problem, then he will quite naturally go into selling mode, albeit more subtle than a double-glazing salesman. He wants new business – all accountants do – and he may help reinforce the doubts you have had with your existing advisor at the same time as building up his own reputation and establishing a rapport with you

He will undoubtedly explain how easy it is to change. You do not need to have any contact with your old accountant – the new one will do it all for you. He may even have a standard letter that he gets you to sign that he will forward to your old accountant. This simply thanks him for his services and gives the name of the new one. The new accountant then writes to the old and gets all your papers, files, books and transfer information sent on by the old accountant. If both accountants are members of either of the two main professional bodies, this process in simple and standard. If you have only ever seen your old accountant say once a year there is no problem whatsoever. If, however, you have a regular 'financial director' situation where you see your accountant monthly, then things are a bit more complicated by his personal knowledge – but still achievable.

Don't expect your old accountant to be cordial with you: losing a client is a blow to him and his practice and he will not want to waste valuable time on you now you won't be paying him anymore.

He will do what he professionally has to but *no more*.

AND FINALLY

Now you have come to the end of this book of revelations, tips and advice, I hope you are well prepared to deal with your accountant. That you can make more sound judgements on service and fees. And, in the end that you now have that good accountant acting for you.

Perhaps you might like to keep this book for future reference - and dare I say it, recommend it to your friends and anybody who uses an accountant. You can contact me at the email below. I would welcome your comments and queries.

Good luck, work with your accountant and prosper !

chrisrowlandthomas@gmail.com

20

GOOD OR BAD?

So let's take a light-hearted test to see how your guy comes out. Put your answer in the table at the end to see how many points your accountant scores. Pick the letter that would be closest to your answer.

Q1   How did you find your accountant?

   a) Recommendation   b) advert   c) met by chance d) other

Q2   How were your fees quoted?

   a)In writing   b) verbally   c) not at all   d) other

Q3   How many years do you think he has been in practice?

   a) One   b) two to five   c) five to ten   d) over ten

Q4   Does he give the impression of serious knowledge?

   a) All the time   b) occasionally   c) not really   d) don't know

Q5   Does he send you out a tax return letter?

a) Always   b) sometimes   c) no   d) not applicable

Q6   How does he return your calls?

a) Fast   b) slow   c) average   d) not applicable

Q7   How does he return your emails?

a) Fast   b) slow   c) average   d) not applicable

Q8   Has a visit to you been done?

a) Never   b) once   c) over once   d) not relevant

Q9   Do you have a mobile number?

a) Yes, for him   b) for one of his staff   c) no   d) he does not have one

Q10   Does he raise the question of lowering your tax?

a) Often   b) never   c) don't know   d) occasionally

Q11   Has he shown proactivity?

a) You must be joking   b) occasionally   c) very much   d) other

Q12   Have you ever had a fine?

a) Never   b) once   c) more than once   d) don't know

Q13   Have you ever been charged interest?

a) Never b) once c) more than once d) don't know

Q14   Have you ever had a VAT assessment?

a) Never   b) once   c) more than once   d) don't know

Q15 Have you ever been investigated by HMRC?

a) Never   b) once   c) more than once   d) don't know

Q16 Has he commented on your bookkeeping?

a) Never   b) occasionally   c) always   d) don't know

Q17 Do you get reminders for tax or accounts?

a) Always   b) never   c) not needed   d) don't know

Q18 Do you get told your tax liability in advance?

a) Never   b) occasionally   c) always   d) don't know

Q19 Have you ever considered changing accountants?

a) Never   b) once   c) more than once   d) don't know

Q20 How enthusiastic is he?

a) Super   b) lacklustre   c) normal   d) other

Q21 Do you know anything about his family?

a) Nothing   b) he has photos on desk   c) basics d) other

Q22 Is he a member of a professional body?

a) Chartered   b) Certified   c) don't know   d) no

Q23 How organised is his office?

a) Incredible   b) good   c) files everywhere   d) bad

Q24   Does he file on line?

a) Don't know   b) must do   c) yes   d) other

Q25   How does he dress?

a) Snappy   b) normal   c) toff   d) scruffy

Q26   Would he visit you in jail for tax fraud?

a) Not in a million years   b) maybe   c) stupid question   d) yes

Q27   Are you kept waiting to see him?

a) Usually   b) if on phone   c) never   d) other

Q28   Does he wear glasses?

a) Sometimes   b) never   c) don't know   d) other

Q29   Does he like talking?

a) Yes   b) no   c) technically   d) other

Q30   Does he listen?

a) Carefully   b) sort of   c) not the best   d) other

Q31   How would you describe his office?

a) OTT   b) back room   c) normal   d) other

Q32   Have you had a letter of engagement?

a) Yes   b) no   c) don't know   d) other

Q33   Did he ask for your passport?

a) Yes   b) no   c) don't know   d) other

Q34 How would you assess the level of fees charged?

a) Fair   b) too high   c) too low   d) other

Q35 Does he have support staff?

a) Yes   b) no   c) don't know   d) other

Q36 Does the firm have a website?

a) Yes   b) no   c) don't know   d) other

Q37 Have you been aware of any errors?

a) Yes   b) no   c) don't know   d) other

Q38 Do his bills come as surprises?

a) Yes   b) no   c) don't know   d) other

Q39 Have you ever had suggestions for director's loan account?

a) Yes   b) no   c) don't know   d) other

Q40 Has the question of your trading vehicle ever been raised?

a) Yes   b) no   c) don't know   d) other

Q41 Do you feel like a favoured client?

a) Yes   b) no   c)   don't know   d) other

Q42 Has he recommended you to a financial advisor?

a) Yes   b) no   c) don't know   d) other

Q43 Do you go to his office?

a) Never   b) if asked   c) yes   d) other

Q44 Do the accounts come to you in bound covers?

a) Yes   b) no   c) don't know   d) other

Q45 **Do you get asked to sign accounts and returns?**

a) Yes   b) no   c) don't know   d) other

Q46 **How comic do you regard him as?**

a) No sense of humour   b) average   c) funny   d) other

Q47 **How long have you been with him?**

a) Less than 1yr   b) 1-5   c) 5-10   d) over 10

Q48 **Does he make use of a secretary?**

a) Yes   b) no   c) don't know   d) other

Q49 **Does he ask after your family?**

a) Yes b) no c) don't know d) other

Q50 **What car does he drive?**

a) Don't know   b) flash   c) ordinary   d) other

TAKE THE MARKS FOR YOUR CHOICE

Q1	a) 2	b) 0	c) 0	d) 1	......
Q2	a) 2	b) 1	c) 0	d) 0	......
Q3	a) 0	b) 0	c) 1	d) 2	......
Q4	a) 2	b) 1	c) 0	d) 0	......
Q5	a) 2	b) 0	c) 0	d) 1	......
Q6	a) 2	b) 0	c) 1	d) 0	......
Q7	a) 2	b) 1	c) 1	d) 0	......
Q8	a) 0	b) 1	c) 2	d) 1	......
Q9	a) 2	b) 1	c) 0	d) 0	......
Q10	a) 2	b) 0	c) 0	d) 1	......
Q11	a) 0	b) 2	c) 0	d) 0	......
Q12	a) 2	b) 0	c) 0	d) 0	......
Q13	a) 2	b) 0	c) 0	d) 0	......
Q14	a) 2	b) 0	c) 0	d) 0	......
Q15	a) 2	b) 0	c) 0	d) 0	......
Q16	a) 0	b) 1	c) 2	d) 0	......
Q17	a) 0	b) 1	c) 2	d) 0	......
Q18	a) 0	b) 1	c) 2	d) 0	......
Q19	a) 2	b) 0	c) 0	d) 0	......
Q20	a) 1	b) 0	c) 2	d) 0	......
Q21	a) 0	b) 0	c) 2	d) 0	......
Q22	a) 1	b) 1	c) 0	d) 0	......
Q23	a) 2	b) 1	c) 0	d) 0	......
Q24	a) 1	b) 1	c) 2	d) 1	......

Q25	a) 0	b) 2	c) 0	d) 1	......
Q26	a) 0	b) 0	c) 2	d) 0	......
Q27	a) 0	b) 1	c) 2	d) 0	......
Q28	a) 2	b) 1	c) 0	d) 0	......
Q29	a) 1	b) 0	c) 1	d) 1	......
Q30	a) 1	b) 0	c) 2	d) 0	......
Q31	a) 0	b) 1	c) 2	d) 0	......
Q32	a) 2	b) 0	c) 0	d) 0	......
Q33	a) 2	b) 0	c) 0	d) 0	......
Q34	a) 2	b) 1	c) 0	d) 0	......
Q35	a) 2	b) 0	c) 0	d) 0	......
Q36	a) 2	b) 0	c) 0	d) 0	......
Q37	a) 1	b) 2	c) 0	d) 0	......
Q38	a) 1	b) 2	c) 0	d) 0	......
Q39	a) 0	b) 2	c) 0	d) 0	......
Q40	a) 2	b) 0	c) 1	d) 1	......
Q41	a) 2	b) 0	c) 1	d) 1	......
Q42	a) 0	b) 2	c) 1	d) 1	......
Q43	a) 0	b) 1	c) 2	d) 1	......
Q44	a) 2	b) 0	c) 1	d) 1	......
Q45	a) 2	b) 0	c) 1	d) 1	......
Q46	a) 1	b) 2	c) 1	d) 1	......
Q47	a) 0	b) 0	c) 1	d) 2	......
Q48	a) 1	b) 2	c) 1	d) 1	......
Q49	a) 2	b) 1	c) 1	d) 1	......
Q50	a) 1	b) 0	c) 2	d) 0	......

I was once recommended to a famous Hollywood actor for his UK income and the first question he asked the recommender was:

'What car does the accountant drive?'

His crazy evaluation – now try yours

Your accountant is:	80–100	Excellent
	60–80	Good
	40–60	Average
	20–40	Dismal
	0–20	Bad

YOUR TOTAL IS ....

Printed in Great Britain
by Amazon